see all the PEOPLE under the steeple

JACOB D. EPPINGA

CRC Publications
Grand Rapids, Michigan

Cover illustration: Laurie Sienkowski

See All the People Under the Steeple, © 1999 by CRC Publications, 2850 Kalamazoo Ave. SE, Grand Rapids, MI 49560.

We welcome your comments. Call 1-800-333-8300 or e-mail us at editors@crcpublications.org.

Library of Congress Cataloging-in-Publication Data
Eppinga, Jacob D., 1917-
    See all the people: (under the steeple) / Jacob D. Eppinga.
       p. cm.
    ISBN 1-56212-498-6
       1. Christian biography—United States. I. Title.

    BR1700.2.E66 1999
    277.3'082'0922—dc21

                                    99-044630

10 9 8 7 6 5 4 3 2 1

Contents

A Grand Mix 5

1. It's a Small, Small World 11

2. A Mind Is a Wonderful Thing 19

3. The Catechism Lesson 25

4. My Gas Station Friend 31

5. The Wall 35

6. Old Sermons 41

7. The Blanket 47

8. Liberal-Conservative 53

9. A Very Long Stairway 59

10. Pinkie 67

11. The Cucumber Lady 75

12. Three Bucks 83

13. The Visitor 89

14. Tom, Dick, and Harry 97

15. Hospitality 117

16. This Is a Church—This Is a Steeple 133

17. O Day of Rest and Gladness 145

    I Love Thy Church, O Lord 159

A Grand Mix

This is a church.
This is a steeple.
Open the doors.
See all the people!

These words are from a children's game. You may have played it with a child. Perhaps your parents played it with you when you were small. I learned it from my father when I began to talk. The motions that accompany the words are—short of a demonstration—difficult to explain. But let me try.

This is a church.
Put your hands together, palms inward, with interlocking fingers not outside but inside the palms of your hands. It takes some imagination to believe that what you are now seeing is a church. It certainly doesn't look like Gothic or New England architecture. But then, lots of churches these days don't look like churches.

Someone once observed that conservative evangelical congregations often erect houses of worship with modern, even futuristic designs, while those that hold to a more liberal theology tend to build sanctuaries in a traditional style. Interesting! Is there some conclusion to be drawn from this observation?

At any rate, your interlocking fingers inside your palms, which by this time are beginning to feel uncomfortable, certainly do not resemble a church. But no matter. Children have good imaginations.

This is a steeple.

Extract the two forefingers from inside your palms and leave the other fingers in place. Straighten the forefingers upwards and let their tips touch.

This is more like it. The forefingers now resemble a steeple. Sort of. Most people associate churches with steeples. Christmas cards depicting churches never show them without steeples. Steeples are churches' distinguishing feature. Congregations whose funds are limited build short, stumpy ones. These are really cupolas. It's the tall spires, however, that catch our eye. These speak, in architectural language, of heavenly aspirations, of reaching for God. They are often set on an octagonal base, representing the eight attributes of God. These octagons rest, in turn, on a square base, representing the foursquare city of which we read in the last book of the Bible.

None of this is evident in your two forefingers sticking up and touching. Even so, what you now have does resemble the vague outline of a church. Sort of.

Open the doors.

Your thumbs, which are the doors to your church, should be parallel to and touching each other under the arch created by your forefingers. They seem to be too large for the dimensions of your church. Never mind. If it bothers you, just think of those huge, ancient cathedral doors in Europe. What should bother you more is that, because of the bone structure of your hands, you can't open your thumbs the way we open doors. Just pretend, therefore, that the hinges are on the bottom and not the sides, as you thrust your thumbs outward towards your face.

What you now have is a church with an open door. Alas, not all churches have this feature. I remember the story of a very race-conscious town where a black man was denied entrance into a white man's church. On the way out he met Jesus Christ, who commiserated with him, saying that he, too, had been trying unsuccessfully for years to gain admittance. It is a story with a point. It is still true in our land that the most segregated hour in the week is the Sunday morning worship hour. As it is also still sadly true that there are churches where the gospel message is not heard.

But let's get back to your thumbs thrust outward and representing the open doors of your church. Take a moment to contemplate them. Let them symbolize the great invitation: "Come unto me all ye who are weary and heavy laden . . . "

See all the people.

Now peer through your open thumbs, or doors. Inside there will be revealed to you six fingers. Wiggle them. They represent the people inside your church.

What do you see? Two pinkies, which are short; two middle fingers, which are tall; and two ring fingers, which, as my piano teacher told me years ago, are the weakest of all.

In the real church it is no different. See all the people! A grand mix. Among God's people there are no two alike. Siblings may resemble one another. But in God's family the brothers and sisters bear traits of many nations and races. Black and yellow, brown and white, and all are precious in his sight.

Many years ago, Dr. Clarence Bouma, a Calvin Seminary professor in Grand Rapids, Michigan, visited with Dr. D. Martin Lloyd Jones, who was the minister of Westminster Chapel in London, England. Both, of course, spoke English, albeit with different accents, as they conversed on matters ecclesiastical and theological.

Dr. Bouma was a member of a denomination that excluded lodge members for reasons that need not be mentioned here. He inquired of Dr. Jones what his view on the matter was, and whether he had lodge members in his chapel. The latter was greatly puzzled by the question. He thought it was a peculiar one. After a moment of reflection, Dr. Jones replied, "Well, as a matter of fact we do have lodge (large) members, small ones too, and many in-between sizes." Of course, the misunderstanding came about by way of a difference in tongue, or, as George Bernard Shaw loved to say, the difference between the English language and the American dialect.

But yes! See all the people. Some are tall, some are short, and many are in between. Some are tall in the faith—the pillars of the church. Others are pinkie-small, like children, and some are ring-finger-weak, needing more fiber in their faith. Some are likable, others less so. The first church of the twelve was a grand mix. Peter was impetuous, Thomas was from

A Grand Mix

Missouri—the "show me" state—and John was a man to whom anyone could entrust his mother.

Having stood in pulpits for over fifty years, I have had a view of them all: the rich and the poor, the schooled and the unschooled, the young and the old, the polished and the diamonds in the rough.

In his letter to the Galatians, Paul writes that in Christ we are neither Jew nor Greek, neither slave nor free, neither male nor female—we are all one in Christ. This is gloriously true. And yet, within the body of the church, some are Jews and others Greeks. And some are slaves and others free. And some are men and some are women. Within our unity there is great diversity. So it was, and is still. Middle fingers. Ring fingers. Pinkies. Just look past your open thumbs.

In the stories that follow I hope to "open the doors" and introduce you to some of the people that are in the sketchbook I carry around with me in my head. The people you will read about here are real people who really lived, though most of them have since moved into the nearer presence of their Lord. They illustrate the great diversity of people we find 'under the steeple,' and they have all enriched my life in one way or another.

May they enrich yours as well.

It's a Small, Small World

His overcoat, which swallowed him whole, dragged behind him on the sidewalk like a bridal train. A huge Texas-type hat, which came down to his ears, made his shrunken face appear to be even smaller than it was. He was a sight people failed to miss. Everything about him was tiny.

I introduced myself to him. I asked for his name. He said, "People call me Hezekiah."

I was the new pastor of a church in downtown Grand Rapids, Michigan. The members lived mostly in the suburbs. With three hospitals within walking distance, I soon became aware of another congregation within the shadows of our tower, made up in part of folks we call "street people."

Every city has them. The wanderers. The unemployed. The winos and the druggies. Older people with broken dreams. Younger people down on their luck. There were all kinds and types, mostly men. They slept under bridges, over warm grates in wintry weather, in fleabag hotels, or at the rescue mission. Some knocked on our doors for handouts.

I decided to become a street person myself for a few hours every Thursday afternoon after the Rotary meeting. That's how I met Hezekiah.

There was a greasy spoon nearby. I took him there for coffee and a conversation. Both were failures. A week later I looked for him. Once more he was my guest, and once more the coffee was terrible and the conversation almost nonexistent. The third week it was the same. The fourth week he was looking for me.

He told me where he lived. Sort of. Across the river somewhere. On the third floor somewhere. I told him that I was a pastor. I said my church was in the next block and that he should come to the service the following Sunday morning at ten o'clock. He said he would, but I knew he wouldn't. That was because his mind seemed to move in and out of a fog. At times he was clear, but there were other moments when he stared at me, trance-like, in suspended animation.

The following Sunday morning, as I was gearing up for the service, there was a knock on my study door. It was the custodian. He told me that there was a little man with a big hat in church and that he was sitting in the front pew. "What should we do?" he asked. "Oh," I said, showing my delight, "that must be Hezekiah!" I went to look, followed by the dubious doorkeeper of the house of the Lord.

It was early, and there were only a few people in church. They were seated in the back pews. Of course! For concerts, people come early for front seats. For church, people come early for the back ones. But way up front I saw a hat. It was a familiar hat. It moved. I knew who was under it.

"Holy, holy, holy." That's one of my favorite hymns with which to begin a service. The sanctuary was filled. There was an overflow crowd in the adjoining parish house. I followed the singing choir down the aisle. The standing congregation added its voice to that of the choir. Only when I ascended the pulpit could I see Hezekiah. When everyone sat down after the invocation, he became visible. He sat solemnly under his hat, his feet dangling like those of a child. They didn't even reach the floor! His hat, though on his head, was no obstruction for the person seated behind him.

The service followed its normal flow until the middle of my sermon. It was then that a most unusual—and most disconcerting—thing happened. Hezekiah slid down from his seat and stood on his feet. It is true that few people noticed this because he was no taller standing up than he was sitting down. He did not rise, to quote G. K. Chesterton, describing a large gentleman of the plastering profession who did the same thing under similar circumstances, "as some leviathan from the deep." Only those seated on both sides of Hezekiah took note. But they were kindly people with poise, and happy to see, as they said later, "someone from the neighborhood in church." Yet they were as startled as I was when my friend fixed me with a stern stare, raised his arm, pointed his finger in my direction, and remained in that position till the end of my homily.

Preaching is *not* as easy as falling off a log. It requires one's utmost. For this reason there must be as few distractions as possible. Ideally, everything must lend itself to the sermon's successful delivery. But my friend Hezekiah seemed unaware, or, at worst, indifferent to such considerations. It was only with some special help from the Lord that I was able to bring the message of the morning to its conclusion. I can testify to classes of seminarians, as I have, about the difficulty of preaching when someone in the first row of pews is standing, pointing at you, and sticking his finger, as it were, in your face.

After the service and numerous handshakes at the door, I was eager to speak with Hezekiah. I expressed my delight at his presence. Anxious to get to my question, I asked, as soon as the moment was opportune, why he had stood and pointed his finger at me. For some reason he seemed less friendly than when we had been together at the greasy spoon. All he said in answer to my question, in a dark manner, was, "You know!" The fact was that I didn't know. Frustration! A deacon took Hezekiah home. It was from the deacon that I learned the exact location of the residence that Hezekiah had told me was "across the river somewhere, and on the third floor somewhere."

On Monday morning I went to his address. As I climbed two long flights of stairs, I wondered how Hezekiah's little legs could carry him that high. He seemed happy to see me and invited me in. I was surprised. His room was unexpectedly large and neat. It was also spare. The single bed was made. Beneath it was an instrument. He called it a zither. A table by the window held a large old book with small print. It was in the Dutch language and written by an author whose name I recognized. "Smytegeld." A few generations earlier, devout Hollanders had regularly digested its contents. Among them, as I learned, was Hezekiah's father.

The table holding Smytegeld yielded further secrets. There were needles and odds and ends of cloth. There were some faded pictures—snapshots of people whose identities he could not remember. My questions brought some answers. He had never been married. He knew a few Dutch words and phrases, but not many. He had been a tailor. Inside the cover of the book was a name. Pieter Z. Hezekiah asked me if I wanted to hear him play his zither. He strummed a bit, enough for me to know that he couldn't really play it at all. But it was his prized possession. I could tell by the way he returned it to its proper place beneath the bed.

Hezekiah, or whatever his name really was, adopted our church. He was present every Sunday. Always in the front pew. On those mornings when he looked unfriendly, I knew that, somewhere along the line, he would stand up and point his finger at me. After a while it didn't bother me anymore. A person can get used to anything. But every time I asked him why he did it, his answer was always an accusing "You know!"

In those days my parents, still living, would occasionally drive over from Detroit for weekend visits. I told them about Hezekiah. I said, "Don't get upset if a little man with a big hat stands up during my sermon and points his finger at me." I added, "Maybe you would like to be seated towards the front Sunday morning so that you can see and also meet him." I told them more—as much as I knew.

On Sunday morning my mother reluctantly followed my father and sat directly behind Hezekiah. I saw that he wore his friendly look. It seemed that the service would progress that day without his pointed finger, and I was right. My father, who spoke with him after the service at some length, couldn't wait to talk to me when I came home. He spoke excitedly. I could hardly believe what he said. I was reminded of the old adage "Truth is stranger than fiction."

"When I grew up in Harlingen, in Holland, there was a family with eight children who lived upstairs from us. My parents had the same number of children. The father, upstairs, was a tailor. His name was Pieter Z. All of his children were small, especially the youngest, whom we referred to as 'Popke' (little doll). He resented his nickname. It made him angry. This resulted in his being mocked all the more." My father paused. Then he wondered out loud. "Could your Hezekiah be our Popke of years ago? His real name was Hendrik. I'd like to see him again."

It seemed impossible. And yet plausible. Hezekiah and Hendrik were names that were not entirely dissimilar. A lot of people in Grand Rapids had come from Holland. And how about that name in his book? Pieter Z.! On Monday morning I dropped my father off at Hezekiah's place while I ran some errands. I picked him up an hour or so later. I could see that my father was excited. He looked at me with widened eyes. He said, "Can you believe it? Hezekiah is Popke! Years and years ago we lived in the same house!" My father couldn't get over it. Neither could I.

During lunch at our house he told us of his visit. He had recognized a few of the pictures. Hezekiah had responded to some words and phrases of the old days. He smiled when my father called him by his right name, Hendrik. "Nobody calls me that anymore," he said.

I interrupted. "But why does he point his finger at me sometimes in the middle of my sermons? And when I ask him why he does this, why does he answer disapprovingly, 'You know,' when I *don't* know?"

My father said, "But I *do* know; I found out." He explained. It was a sad story. "When we were small, we went to the same church. Our minister was every inch a minister. Along with the mayor, he was highly regarded. Highly respected. He had a cane with a golden handle. At least, we thought it was gold. And he had a voice like an organ. People stood up when he came into a room. They stood aside when he walked down the street. But something happened. He was caught in a terrible scandal. He was defrocked. He was deposed. He left town in disgrace. His wife and his housekeeper were never seen again. The whole town and the entire province were stunned. My parents spoke of it in whispers and never when the children were present. Some people were so shaken they never went to church again."

There was a pause. My father looked at me and then continued. "I noticed, just as you told me, that Hendrik has a feeble mind. Sometimes it was clear when we talked. Sometimes it wasn't. Sometimes he lives in the present. Sometimes in the past. Mentally, he's in and out. But when I probed him about the reason for his finger-pointing in church, the fog lifted, and he gave me an answer. When he does it, he thinks you're that minister of long ago."

I didn't know whether to laugh or cry. After a momentary silence, we all began to talk at once. "Imagine! Here is a little old man, daily wandering the streets of Grand Rapids' inner city, sometimes rolled by drunks for the pennies he might have, much of his past forgotten, yet still showing the effects of damage inflicted on him by a minister!" "Remember what Jesus said? Whosoever offends one of these little ones . . . " "How conscious we must be as adults to be good examples to our children!" "When you think of him as small and weak, think what an act of courage it must be on his part to stand up in church and, as it were, unmask the preacher!" "How sad, when he goes to church, that he sometimes grows disturbed, mistaking memory for reality."

There were other observations and remarks. But we couldn't get over the fact that after all these years, these two—my father and Popke (Hendrik-Hezekiah)—should meet again! It's a small, small world.

A few Sundays later, Hendrik, as I now called him, was not in church. We found him ailing and weak. He apologized. He couldn't manage those long flights of stairs anymore. His landlord was kind and helpful. So were the deacons. Arrangements were made. And so it was that, together with my associate, we carried him down those many steps to bring him to the county facility, known in those days as the "poor farm."

Together we wrestled him into the back of my station wagon, where he sat facing the rear. He didn't like that. We turned him around. He said, "That's better," and spoke no more until he had been placed in a clean bed. We came into the room to say goodbye and to put his beloved zither under his bed. He still wore his hat. He spread his painfully thin arms out and pronounced the benediction over us. We bowed our heads. We left with moist eyes.

A few weeks later he died. My father drove in for the funeral. Hardly anyone attended. Just a few of us.

And God!

A month later I brought a needy family to the Salvation Army store to help buy them some clothing. There, hanging from a wall, was Hezekiah's zither! It was for sale.

I am sorry to this day that I didn't buy it.

A Mind Is a Wonderful Thing

The older one was ninety years young. The younger one was eighty-five years old. They were sisters. One was short. The other, the older, lean. They had never married. They had come to America from Holland at ages seven and two. Both had worked all their lives as housekeepers in large and stately homes still standing in an older section of town—homes that had belonged to the lumber barons of a former day. Now the sisters lived in small adjoining houses on a street that no longer exists as, years ago, both street and houses gave way to an expanding hospital facility.

Calling on them as their new pastor, I was warned to observe the pecking order and call on the older sister first. The furnishings in her living room were orderly, and as spare as she was lean. Her hair was pulled up tightly into a bun, which perched like a knot on the top of her head. She was proper, formal, and sat erect. Ninety years had slowed neither her mind nor her step. Knowing that she was born in the old country, I was anxious to display my limited knowledge of her native tongue. To my surprise my efforts fell flat. She had no memory of her ancestral language whatsoever.

She explained. She had left her homeland over eighty years ago and had lived with an English-speaking family and employer until she retired. I sensed a lack of interest in the language subject, even some annoyance with it, and shifted the conversation to something else.

It had occurred to me that two aged sisters, living alone in adjoining houses, ought, instead, to live together. It would be a savings. And think of the companionship! I couldn't imagine why the advantages of sharing the same house had not crossed their minds. The moment after I gave voice to this bright idea, I realized that I had stuck my foot in my mouth again. She was about as receptive to my notion as she had been to discussing her native tongue. She said that it would never work and added that they really didn't get along with each other very well. And that was the end of that subject.

Having been conversationally stonewalled twice, it was obvious that I was not making a very good initial impression as her new pastor. My eyes searched the room for something else to talk about and found, standing on an end table, a small glass replica of a greyhound. It was about four inches tall, semi-transparent, and complete in every detail. The delicate glass legs were perfectly formed and appeared very breakable. I referred to it with admiration. She smiled, warmed towards me, and said it was her prized possession. It was valuable, precious. It was a gift from her former employer.

The ice was broken. We were finally on the same footing. We had something in common. We were both admirers of her glass greyhound. She confided in me and said that she even talked to it sometimes. After a Bible verse and a prayer, I took my leave and went next door.

The younger sister, who looked older, opened to me before I could ring the bell. If she had a trumpet, she would have blown a fanfare. She had seen me enter her sister's house. She wondered how long I would stay there. She wanted to know what we talked about. She picked up her cat from an overstuffed chair and asked me to sit down. As I sat in the cat's chair, I scanned the room. Clutter everywhere. Would I like some tea? And what did I think of her sister? Wasn't she smart?

She said that they communicated every day by using their window shades. If one sister's shade was not up by 10:00 a.m., the other knew that she was sick or needed something. One morning the younger sister forgot to raise her shade. The older sister came right away, so the younger pretended to be sick. Otherwise her sister would have acted put out. She added quickly, however, that they loved each other very much.

The following Sunday I saw them in church together—two more people I could identify in my large new congregation. They always sat in the same place. They came early and left early. When they couldn't walk to church anymore, the transportation committee took over. Then the sisters came later, but the ushers always saved their seats for them. Way in the back.

When finally they couldn't manage the steps, their churchgoing days came to an end. I increased my pastoral calls on "The Sisters," as I referred to them in my mind. The older one first, of course. I'd express my increasing appreciation for the glass greyhound. Then after Scripture, prayer, and the sacrament, I'd go next door where, sitting in the cat's overstuffed chair, I repeated my ministrations. It became a monthly routine. Both sisters looked forward to my calls, and I grew fond of them. The older, who looked younger, was now ninety-five years of age and the younger, who still looked older, had turned ninety. Such longevity!

One day the hospital called to inform me that the older sister had been brought in by ambulance. I rushed there and found the younger sister. She was much concerned. When she saw that her sister's shade was still closed at 10:00 a.m., she went next door. She called the doctor, a member of our church. Though the hospital was practically in the same block, the older sister was taken there by ambulance. I found her gravely ill. She said she was going to die. She asked who was going to take care of her sister.

A few days later the doctor told me that the older sister's condition was terminal. She was moved to a rest home. I called each day. There she was, in the bed, her sister faithfully by her side. It became a familiar scene. Each day she grew weaker. Soon she entered a coma. Despite this fact, I read a verse of Scripture to her each day and also prayed with her. She never responded. She never opened her eyes.

Was it an exercise in futility to read a Scripture verse each day to someone who was comatose? The faithful, ever-present younger sister thought so. "She can't hear you," she said, and added, "She can't hear me either." I was persuaded, indeed, that the patient was beyond reach. Even so, I continued to read a Scripture verse to her and to offer a brief prayer. I had read somewhere that sometimes people in her situation are able to hear even though they do not respond.

A few days before she died, I called again, as was now my custom. The rest home was conveniently located—just a few blocks out of my way when I drove home from church in the late afternoon. There was the younger sister, sitting by the bed, holding the hand of the only one she had in the world. It was a sad sight. There was nothing I could do—a helpless feeling. But I followed my routine. I leaned in close to the patient's ear and said, "The Lord is my shepherd." There was no response. I waited a few moments. Then, for some strange reason, I did an unpremeditated thing. I leaned in close to her ear again and repeated the same words of Psalm 23, only this time in Dutch. I said, *"De Heere is mijn herder"* (The Lord is my shepherd).

As usual there was no response. I exchanged a word or two with the attending sister, who was quietly weeping. Then something happened. Her sister began to stir. We had not seen this for a week or so. It became obvious that she was trying to speak. We were both very still. We heard her whisper. It was unmistakable. She said, *"Mij zal niets ontbreken"* (I shall not want).

It was amazing. She had completed the verse. She had supplied the remainder of Psalm 23:1 in a language she had long forgotten. A mind is a wonderful thing.

Several days later I conducted her funeral. It was easy to select the text for the meditation. She had chosen it for me: "I shall not want."

On a visit to the younger sister a few months later, I learned that she was preparing to move to a retirement home. I sat in the cat seat for the last time (the cat had already moved to a neighbor's house). She said that she had something to give me—something the older sister had wanted me to have. I took it gingerly. Very carefully.

It was the glass greyhound.

The Catechism Lesson

Teaching catechism is not every preacher's cup of tea. Consider, for example, my short friend, Reverend S., who disliked every class he ever taught.

I was about to retire from the active ministry. Only a few more months and I would be an emeritus clergyman. An overcrowded hospital elevator was carrying me to visit a sick parishioner. Pressed against the back of it, and out of view, stood my short friend, who had retired from the ministry the year before. En route to the second floor he made his presence known with a voice too big for someone short of stature. He said, or rather shouted, that he had heard I was being "emeritated." I didn't think that was a word. Nor did I like the feeling of all heads in close proximity to my own turning in my direction, with eyes wondering what was going to happen to me. Emeri-what? Squeezing himself out of the elevator at the second floor, my friend turned around before the doors closed, and shouted, "Just think! No more catechism classes! Yippee!"

Again I felt wondering eyes turning my way in that crowded enclosure. Catechism? A lost word in today's world. And emeri-what? I grew uncomfortable. At the next floor I got off even though I had two more floors to go. As the doors closed behind me I turned around suddenly and faced an elevator full of disappearing strangers. "Yep," I crowed, "emeritated and no more catechism. Yippee!"

I have often wondered what those people thought as they continued their upward journey, if not in life, then in that hospital conveyance.

The fact is that I always enjoyed teaching catechism to the lambs of the fold. It had its rewards. There was that warm feeling, that inner glow, that came when you knew you had taught somebody something. Teachers know what I mean.

I remember a particular class of high schoolers—fifteen or so bright young people who were always present and prepared. I looked forward to my weekly hour with them. It was always a time of mutual benefit. I increased their knowledge while they, unfailingly, lifted my spirits. All but one, that is! He was bigger than I and was only present because his father, who was bigger than he, insisted. He never listened. His body language came through to me loud and clear. Arms folded, legs crossed, he sat sideways in his chair, looking at me over his shoulder as if to say, "I dare you to teach me anything."

If only Bob (which was not his real name) would just stay home! But what kind of wish was that for a preacher, when Bob's parents were pinning their hopes on me to get through, somehow, to their difficult yet beloved son. These were my thoughts one Wednesday evening as I was driving to church to meet my dream class. All but one, that is.

The lesson I had prepared for that particular evening dealt with the doctrine of the providence of God. The Heidelberg Catechism defines it as "the almighty and ever present power of God by which he upholds, as with his hand, heaven and earth and all creatures, and so rules them that leaf and blade, rain and drought, fruitful and lean years, food and drink, health and sickness, prosperity and poverty—all things, in fact, come to us not by chance, but by his fatherly hand."

Of all the statements in the catechism, this was the one which, although I accepted it, I least understood. I had, on occasion, officiated at the funeral of a child who had so much to live for, after which I called on some aged saint in a rest home anxious to die, yet living on interminably. It often made me wonder at the inscrutable ways of the Almighty.

So God's providence was the lesson for the day. All the members of the class were there, including the ever-present Bob. I began the session with prayer. After this, I started the lesson with a question. "When God, in the beginning, created the world, where did he put it?" One bright young lady responded immediately. She said, "In space." It was the answer I had hoped for. "Ah," I said, and responded as I had planned, "But there was no space. In the beginning there was only God, and nothing else, not even space."

I really didn't know what I was talking about, but my class didn't know that. Maybe space, too, along with God, had no beginning—I don't know . . . I wasn't there. Whatever the truth of the matter, I was sure that the members of the class would receive my answer as something they had never thought about.

I was right. They furrowed their brows. They looked at each other inquiringly. I listened to their responses: "I never thought about that." "How can there be such a thing as no space?" "So where did he put it then?" I had been hoping someone would ask this last question. I singled it out. I said, "I don't know the scientific answer to your question, but I have a better one. He put it all—sun, moon, and stars, Earth, and space too—in his hand. And that's where it all is right now. He's got the whole world—and everything else—in his hands."

I asked the members of the class to extend their left arms, palms upward, and to imagine planet Earth resting in their left hand. "Next," I said, "place your right hand somewhere near your face, fingers extended, and pointing in the direction of planet Earth in your left hand. Wiggle, now, your fingers, pointed in the direction of planet Earth, as if you are guiding and directing everything happening there. This is a picture of God's providential activity. And so, to quote the catechism, 'all things come to you not by chance but by his fatherly hand'."

I continued. I said, "Every time you hear the word 'providence,' or the phrase 'God's providential leading or activity' from some pulpit or some person in your company, all you need to do is mentally extend your left arm, hand upward, place your right hand somewhere near your face, and wiggle your fingers in the direction of planet Earth in your left hand—and you will have an idea of what is meant by God's providential activity."

I paused. I asked them all, "Got it?" and all replied, "Got it." All but Bob, that is. He had not been listening. But I had resolved that Bob would learn something from me that night if it was the last thing I ever did.

I addressed him. "Bob," I said, "I'm going to go over all this again, and this time you'd better listen. Because when I am finished, you are going to come up here and I'm going to sit in your chair, and you are going to teach us the doctrine of the providence of God."

It was a risk. I had no assurance that my proposal would meet with success. But I was encouraged by his physical reaction.

What I had said straightened him out quite literally. He sat up from his slouch. He listened as I repeated what I had said. When I finished I walked towards him. For a split second I worried that he wouldn't get up. He did! He walked to the front of the class. He said that when God created the world he put it in his hand and with his other hand he guides us, takes care of us, and directs us, and that this is the providence of God. His performance was a bit halting. Nevertheless, he got it right.

Yippee! I drove home that night with an inner glow teachers sometimes experience when they know that they broke through to someone. At long last I had taught Bob something!

Less than a year later Bob and his parents moved to one of our eastern states. After a few years they faded from my memory. During the first few years a mental picture of Bob floated across my mind occasionally. But after a while, Bob appeared no more.

Ten years later a cultural revolution had swept the land. There was the rock concert at Woodstock, flower children, love-ins, and more. Students at Berkeley carried their notions of the meaninglessness of life out into the streets. Timothy Leary and Alan Ginsburg were influential in making drugs an ideology. In short, there was an upheaval in values from which America has not yet recovered. On the streets of cities and towns young men were making statements with shoulder-length hair.

It was Thursday and I was making my weekly trek, walking from the church to a downtown hotel for a weekly Rotary meeting. I paused to cross a busy intersection.

There I saw a huge truck, a semi, whose burly driver—hair down to his shoulders and with a beard, no doubt, down to his navel—was waiting for the light to change. He was waving an arm in my direction and blowing his horn. Since there was no one behind me I decided that he was looking at me. I didn't know him, as they say, from Adam. I pointed to myself while looking at him inquiringly. He nodded his head—hair, beard, and all—affirmatively. I made a motion with my hands to indicate that I did not know who he was. The light was about to change. But before it did, he leaned his ample self as far as he could out of his cab window. He extended his left arm with his hand palm up. He put his right hand somewhere near his face, fingers extended and wiggling in the direction of his other hand. It was then that recognition dawned. He was holding the whole world in his left hand, and guiding and directing all things with the other. It was Bob! I was dumbstruck. It was Bob! The light changed. He pulled ahead, still looking and smiling at me. I began jumping up and down excitedly. It was Bob!

I never saw him again. But ever since, driving the highways of our land, I try to see the faces of the truck drivers. For somewhere on America's roads there is a big, burly truck driver barreling along who knows the doctrine of the providence of God.

My Gas Station Friend

I am a Protestant minister. But to "open the doors and see all the people" means opening Roman Catholic church doors too. When I do this, I see my gas station friend attending mass.

My father, well-versed in his heritage, told me many stories about the history of his native land. Listening by the fireplace, I could stare into the flames and see it all: Dutch naval victories, the siege of Leyden, the derring-do of William of Orange and such great sea captains and admirals as Piet Hein and Michiel Adriaanzoon De Ruyter. My father also told me about the sixteenth century, when the Spanish Duke of Alva ruled the Netherlands with an iron fist. Protestants were hounded, persecuted, and killed. Many who would not convert to Roman Catholicism were bound and drowned in Dutch canals. These stories, part of his nation's history, fired my father's soul and made him all the more a child of the Reformation.

Me too! When my father balanced the score a bit and told me of times when Protestants, having the upper hand, chased Roman Catholics, and Calvinists took out against Arminians, I tended to find excuses. I was a fervent Protestant Calvinist at the tender age of twelve. My friend Eddy, who was Polish and

31

Roman Catholic, lived a block away. We argued our differences as two young theologians and sometimes came to blows. I remember telling him one day when he had me down, that if everybody in the whole world turned Roman Catholic, I would be the very last.

Years later I met another Ed. He was Polish too, Roman Catholic too, and my gas station man. It was just like years before. Déjà vu. Ed and I argued our differences, but this time there were no fisticuffs. In time my Polish gas station friend softened somewhat in his partisan opinions. He had grown up on the west side of Grand Rapids, Michigan, where Dutch Protestants and Polish Roman Catholics, although both clean and industrious, mixed like oil and water. After getting to know me and like me, a Protestant minister, Ed reassessed his prejudices. And when he told me that Jesus was his Lord and Savior, I too began to soften.

Meanwhile I was drinking an occasional cup of coffee with Father Poppell, priest at St. Andrews, which was two blocks from my church. We were joined sometimes by Father Michael Beahan, whose popular "Fifteen with Father" drew many TV viewers. These conversations served to widen my mind and make me more tolerant. At the same time I found myself more deeply rooted in my own convictions. I told both priests, like I had told a young friend years before, that if everybody in the world turned Roman Catholic, I would be the very last. I also told them of one of their fellow Roman Catholics, namely Ed, my gas station man, whom I was trying to convert to Protestantism.

Poppell and Beahan versus Eppinga. How different we were! And yet there was a bond—aided by a sense of humor. My congregation had just decided to raze our old church building and to replace it with a new structure at the same location. With tongue in cheek I asked my Roman Catholic counterparts for a donation to our building fund. Father Beahan said that his principles forbade such a gift but that he would be happy to contribute to the tearing-down of our old structure.

Some time later, both priests arranged for me to give a lecture to the nurses at St. Mary's Hospital on the Protestant view of the sacrament of baptism. Furthermore, I was invited to participate in the ceremonies to dedicate the hospital's new wing, and, on three occasions, I was invited to give the commencement addresses for the graduating nurses. Meanwhile, I kept working on Ed, my gas station friend, and making what I thought was some progress in getting him to walk through our church doors.

Ed was a member of the Polish Heritage Society. I was a member of The Dutch Immigrant (now International) Society. To show their mutual love for America, the great melting pot, both societies decided to organize an unprecedented joint patriotic celebration. I was asked to chair this effort. That's how I met the late Father Snigowski, pastor of St. Adalbert's Cathedral, deep in the heart of West Side Polish territory. Father Snigowski was Ed's pastor. We decided to hold an interfaith service at St. Adalbert's. Father Snigowski asked me to preach the sermon.

On a bitterly cold February evening, the event took place. Despite the weather, the cathedral was filled to capacity. I had asked the resident Father if he would permit me to preach on the first question and answer of our catechism—The Heidelberg Catechism:

Q: What is your only comfort in life and in death?

A: That I am not my own,
but belong—
body and soul,
in life and in death—
to my faithful Savior Jesus Christ. . . .

The reverend Father, having read this passage, thoroughly approved. Ed, my gas station friend, sat in the front pew. He had said that he would be rooting for me. The next morning I pulled up to one of his pumps. Ed came rushing out. He shook my hand. He congratulated me. To think that his Protestant preacher friend had stood in and preached from the pulpit of his church! I got out of the car. He patted me on my back and gave me his opinion of my message.

"Reverend," he said, "it was a damn good sermon!"

A few years later my gas station friend was stricken with cancer. I called on him frequently and spoke of Jesus, the only way to heaven. When he was nearing the end, he called for me. I came late at night. He wanted me to say a prayer. I went to the hospital and found him weak but still the same old Ed. "Rev.," he said, "I've pumped your last gallon. But keep going and don't run out of gas." Then he asked me for a prayer. We were alone. His family had temporarily left the room so we could speak together. I read a few Scripture verses. I prayed. I pronounced the benediction. I said goodbye to my friend.

As I left the room, a priest walked in. He was there to administer extreme unction, the last rites of the Catholic church. I turned, surprised, for a last look at Ed. He smiled a holy smile. "Now," he said, "I got double insurance—a preacher *and* a priest."

The old gas station is no more. It has been replaced by a modern self-service establishment. I still go there. Sometimes, pumping my own gas now, I think of Ed. I got him halfway into my church. But I'm sure he's all the way into heaven.

After all, he said that he believed in Jesus as his Savior and Lord.

The Wall

People who sit on church building committees are not always qualified to do so. The story is told of an immigrant just off the boat. He knew little about construction and even less of the English language. But the church he joined had a limited membership, which meant that everybody had to put his shoulder to the wheel. So this man was put on the building committee.

At a congregational meeting it was decided to purchase a new chandelier for the sanctuary because the illumination was deemed inadequate for worship. The matter was referred to the building committee. Its newest member—the one just off the boat—was against the proposition. With a foreign accent and in broken English, he gave three reasons for his opposition to the chandelier. In the first place, he said, he didn't think anyone in the congregation could spell it. In the second place, he didn't think that there was anyone in the congregation who could play it. And in the third place, he added, "What we really need around here is more light."

The building committee in my church consisted of more knowledgeable members. When their three-year terms of service expired, there were always enough qualified persons to take their places. And so, serving my church for almost thirty-four years, I saw building committee members come and go.

The matter of long versus short pastorates, incidentally, is often debated. Some say that ministers should move every ten to twelve years. Others maintain that ministers' terms should be shorter. Others believe that, if things are going well, long-term pastorates are preferable. It is hard to make a ruling on this matter. So much depends on individual circumstances.

My third pastorate turned out to be much longer than the average. Over a span of three decades and more, I learned not only to love my parishioners, but to identify with them. Baptizing infants whose parents or *grand*parents I had married brought with it a family closeness impossible to experience in a short term of service. Long pastorates can bring other insights as well. For example:

The second floor of the parish house held classrooms on both sides of a long center hall. The classrooms were all of equal size and adequate for church school functions. However, some members of the education committee felt that there was a need for one larger room. This room could be created by removing one wall, thus making one larger room in the place of two smaller ones. The matter was referred by the church council to the building committee for study and recommendation. Was it structurally possible? How much would it cost? Which of the walls could be removed most easily? Should the work be done by volunteers or should a contractor be engaged? If the latter, which contractor?

The building committee, having done its homework in admirable fashion, brought its recommendation for the removal of a wall to the ruling body. Questions were asked and answered. After a thorough discussion, pro and con, the recommendation passed by a majority vote. The education committee members were happy. Soon the upstairs of the parish house had a room of double size.

Ten years later all the members of the education and building committees who had decided to remove the wall had long since been replaced. At a meeting of the church council, the education committee submitted a request. There was need for an additional classroom on the second floor of the parish house. This classroom could be obtained by dividing the larger room into two rooms by building a wall down the middle. Since the larger room was not really needed, there would be no loss. After much discussion and debate, the request was tentatively approved, pending a feasibility study by the building committee. Was it structurally possible? How much would it cost? Could it be done with volunteer work or should a contractor be engaged? If the latter, which contractor?

The building committee, having made a thorough study, brought its recommendation to the church council for the installation of a wall to divide the larger room on the upper level of the parish house into two rooms. Questions were asked and answered. After a lengthy discussion, pro and con, the recommendation of the building committee was presented for a vote.

Before the vote occurred, someone rose to a point of order. The education committee had already brought a similar recommendation to the church council at an earlier meeting. This recommendation had been accepted pending a feasibility study by the building committee. After much discussion, pro and con, the education committee's earlier recommendation was placed before the house, revoted, and carried by a majority vote. Everyone felt good when they left the meeting. The King's business had not been taken lightly.

As chair of this meeting, I experienced an eerie feeling. Few, if any, were aware that we were reinventing a wall that had disappeared a decade before. But I said nothing, mindful of the fact that church council members do not always take kindly to history lessons.

Ten years later all the members of the education and building committees of a decade before who had decided to rebuild the wall had long since been replaced. At a meeting of the church council, the education committee submitted a request. There was a need to enlarge one of the classrooms on the upper level of the parish house. Such a larger space could be obtained by removing one of the walls separating the classrooms. The matter was referred to the building committee for study and recommendation. Was it structurally possible? How much would it cost? Which of the walls could most easily be removed? Should volunteer workers be sought, or should a contractor be used? If the latter, which contractor?

The building committee, having upheld a tradition of doing its work in an admirable manner, brought its recommendation for the removal of a wall to the ruling body. Questions were asked and answered. After a lengthy discussion, pro and con, the recommendation of the building committee passed by a majority vote.

No one but I was aware of the fact that we were dealing with a wall that had been removed twenty years before. I had another strong impulse to make a historical observation, yet stifled it once more. And so it is that a minister in a long pastorate can witness things that cannot be observed in a short space of time—like seeing a wall come down, go up, and come down again.

After another decade, did the wall go up again? No. The whole parish house came down. The education committee needed more classrooms. Other societies needed more space. The whole matter was referred to the building committee for a feasibility study. Its recommendation was that the parish house be razed and replaced. This was done. The new facility is very ample. But having served there a long time, I believe that one of these days more alterations are bound to come.

Old Sermons

My college English professor took me aside. He had some advice to give. "If you're going to be a minister someday, don't go to the same church every Sunday. Visit other churches. Study the styles of as many ministers as possible." He recommended a few. There was a Methodist minister downtown—a real pulpiteer! And there was another, a seminary professor, with a silver tongue and a golden voice.

The following Sunday, I went to hear the real pulpiteer. It was only a two-mile walk. He not only lived up to my professor's praise, but he proved to me that he could handle an emergency. In the middle of his message, a large woman sitting two rows ahead of me fainted. The pulpiteer, seeing his stricken parishioner, immediately interrupted himself and asked that all heads be bowed in a moment of prayer while several men struggled valiantly to carry the woman out of the sanctuary. Walking back to my room after the service, I marveled at the preacher's presence of mind. He had handled the situation just right. I made a mental note. Should a similar situation ever arise during my future ministry, I would handle it with admirable wisdom, just like the Methodist minister. Lamentably, after what is now a fifty-year ministry, no one has ever fainted during any of my services.

A few weeks later I learned that the seminary professor, the one with the silver tongue and the golden voice, would be preaching in a church on the other side of town. I was determined to hear him, despite the fact that it would be about a four-mile hike. I must have been a pretty good kid. I got up earlier than usual that Sunday and covered the four miles in good time. Despite the fact that the church was filling up from the back, I headed for the front. I wanted to have a good look at Dr. Silver Tonsils with the golden sound. Soon he appeared. There was an aura about him. He conducted the service with warmth and dignity. The Scripture reading was from Paul's epistle to the Galatians, the second chapter. The sermon began.

"My text," he said, "is taken from Galatians 2:20: ' . . . the Son of God who loved me and gave himself for me.'" I sat spellbound as he enlarged on his theme. As I traveled the four miles back to my room, I walked on air. That afternoon I wrote a letter to my parents. I told them of the preacher I had heard, and what he had said, and how I couldn't wait to hear him again.

Again a few weeks later my pulpit hero was going to preach in a church near the campus. I looked forward to the service and made sure I was on time. Again I sat in one of the forward pews, the better to see and hear the greatest preacher since Spurgeon. The liturgy was the same as two weeks before. Then came the Scripture reading. It was from Paul's Epistle to the Galatians, the second chapter. The sermon began.

"My text," he said, "is taken from Galatians 2:20: ' . . . the Son of God who loved me and gave himself for me.'" Word for word, it was the same sermon I had heard a few weeks before. I was surprised. It had somehow never occurred to me before that preachers reused their sermons. I was disappointed. Still, I could find nothing unethical about repeating a sermon. And as I listened, I discovered new insights. It was like seeing a movie twice and catching stuff that didn't register the first time around.

When Thanksgiving break came along, I caught a ride to my hometown 180 miles away. My home church was without a minister. With its pulpit vacant, elders were sometimes called upon to read a sermon out of a book of approved sermons found inside the pulpit. Boring! We went to church Thanksgiving morning and, wouldn't you know it, we had no preacher. One of the elders, a poor choice because he read haltingly and nasally, read a sermon that came as close as possible to the subject of thanksgiving. Boring.

As I sat there, I thought of an incident my father had told me about. It happened when I was an infant, sitting on my father's lap in church. An elder was reading a sermon. It was long and deep. Everyone, including the elder, was anxious for it to be over. But after the elder had finished reading the second-to-last page of the sermon, he inadvertently turned two pages instead of one. This landed him on the second page of the next sermon in the book.

Nobody noticed the abrupt change in subject—neither the elder who was reading, nor the congregation which was, presumably, listening. On and on went the sermon. Interminable! As he turned the pages, the elder surreptitiously peeked ahead to see if the end might be just a page more away. It wasn't. But he read on while a passive, suffering congregation bore it all—except one of its members—me! I began to fidget, cry, and bawl, as any infant might after having to sit for a prolonged period of time. My father said it was one time when a crying baby spoke for all.

I came out of my reverie. The sermon reading had come to a merciful end and was followed by an electrifying announce-ment. The following Sunday we would be led in worship by one of our seminary professors. Guess who? The man with the silver tongue and the golden voice! I felt more than pleased. My hero in my home church! I told my father that he had a treat in store. I told my mother to be sure that she didn't have one of her headaches. On the following Sunday morning I was the one, for a change, hurrying everyone along so that we would get to the church on time.

Soon there appeared, coming through a door to one side of the pulpit, that familiar face followed by a string of elders and deacons. The liturgy was the same in our church as those I attended while at college. There was the reading of the Ten Commandments, the pastoral prayer, the offering, and the singing. I was impatient for the sermon to begin. We were up to the Scripture lesson. It was from Paul's letter to the Galatians, the second chapter. The sermon began.

"My text," he said, "is taken from Galatians 2:20: ' . . . the Son of God who loved me and gave himself for me.'" I knew the next sentence, too, and the next. I was hearing it all for a third time, and with a degree of disappointment.

Over the years, I have on occasion reflected on this triple exposure to Galatians 2:20. I have decided that the Lord, in his providence, arranged for me to hear this message three times. Repetition has its merits. Galatians 2:20 and its message have been indelibly impressed on me, to my spiritual profit. I have furthermore come to see that good sermons should not die in preacher's files. In my own barrel there are a few that are passable, and I preach them now and then.

Still, there is a humorous side for those who hear sermons they have heard before. There is the story of a woman who was visiting in a strange town. A friend called at her motel on Sunday morning and took her to church. Reverend Farthington, an itinerant and less-than-stellar preacher, supplied the pulpit that morning. He preached a sermon on Simon Peter's mother-in-law who was ill. Later that afternoon, the woman walked from her motel to a nearby church that had an afternoon service. To her surprise, there was Reverend Farthington again. He preached, once more, on Simon Peter's mother-in-law who was ill.

The sermon was no better the second time around, and the woman regretted the impulse that had brought her to that afternoon service. She looked forward to the invitation extended by some other friends to visit with them at their home over a light lunch before the evening service. She thought it would be pleasant, even a relief, to hear some other preacher that day, having been overdosed on the subject of Simon Peter's mother-in-law's illness. Her friends told her that she would enjoy their minister that evening; Reverend Bradbury was great.

But, alas, Reverend Bradbury didn't appear. It was announced that he had to go to the mountains because of his hay fever. In his place they were fortunate to have obtained the services of Reverend Farthington who was visiting in the area. And so, for a third time that day, the women heard about Simon Peter's mother-in-law who was ill.

Going home on the train the following morning, there was Reverend Farthington, a few seats ahead. She went up to him. She spoke to him. She said, "I suppose Simon Peter's mother-in-law is dead by now. After all, she had a terribly high fever three times yesterday."

The Blanket

My first church was very small. With limited numbers, it was possible to strengthen "the tie that binds" with each member of the congregation. In the course of a year, I could visit every home more than once. But in a large church, as someone once observed, the only way to get to know the preacher is to get sick. I could not give individual attention to all. But the shut-ins saw me once a month, and I visited hospital patients on an almost daily basis.

One of these patients was a woman I didn't know well. After Sunday services we always shook hands and exchanged pleasantries, but when she landed in the hospital for minor repairs, we talked in depth. After a few of these conversations I sensed something of her spiritual strength. I also discovered that she was a reader, and so, a kindred spirit. There is always a special bond—a kinship—between readers. We became a kind of book club, just the two of us. We recommended titles and authors to each other after church or at society meetings.

She was a widow, childless, and in her late sixties. She lived in her own house and was popular with the neighbors, especially the children whom she spoiled with her cookies. She was quite ordinary in appearance. A stranger would not notice her in a crowd. But she was special. She could engage in small talk, but conversations with her soon led to bigger things—like ideas.

In her early seventies, she was diagnosed with cancer. She took the news in stride. She developed a deeper interest in the Old Testament psalms, explaining, "They take on broader dimensions when you are terminal." She submitted to prescribed treatments but gradually weakened. The upstairs bed was moved into the living room by neighbors and members of the church. It was easier for her. No more steps to climb. On my way home I dropped by to see her in the late afternoon two or three times a week. There was always a book or two on her bed and, of course, her Bible. We both enjoyed these moments together, sharing a few thoughts, a verse or two from Scripture, and a prayer.

One day as I was about to leave, my hand on the handle of her front door, she called me back as if to ask me a question. But she changed her mind. "It's too silly to mention," she said. But she wiped away a tear as she dismissed the thought and the impulse to share it. All that evening I kept wondering. What was it that she had withheld? I was bitten by the curiosity bug.

On the next visit I asked her what it was that she had decided was too silly to mention. I said we were good friends and that she could ask her pastor anything, even if it seemed inconsequential. I would not have persisted in prodding her had it not been for that tear. After pressing her on several more visits, she finally told me. "But," she said, "promise not to laugh."

I promised.

I sat down. She took a deep breath. What followed was quite a story. She told me that she had grown up on a farm in a small community nearby. Her childhood had been a happy one in that God had given her the most wonderful mother in the world. It was her mother who had taught her to love books. But when she was ten years old her mother died very suddenly. The church was filled to capacity for the funeral. Afterward they went to the cemetery for the graveside committal. As the minister offered the final prayer, my friend shivered in her thin coat, for it was winter and there was much snow.

When the preacher had finished, and her father and all the relatives and friends returned to their buggies, it finally dawned on her that her mother would be left behind in the cold, cold ground. She broke down and refused to leave. She had to be carried away while struggling and protesting with flailing arms and legs. All that night she couldn't sleep as she thought of her mother, alone, in the dark and wintry cemetery, buried under all that snow.

"All my life," she said, "I have never liked snow. It always reminds me of when my mother died. And now my life is ending. I know it doesn't make any difference what time of the year I die. Just the same, I pray every night that God will take me in the summertime. I'd just as soon not die in winter like my mother did."

"There," she said, "so now you know my secret. I've never told it to anyone else. Silly, isn't it? I won't hold it against you if you laugh."

"I'm not laughing," I said. "I promised I wouldn't, and I won't." I offered the usual prayer and added a request that God would grant her wish. We said our goodbye.

I was thinking about our conversation on my way home when a brilliant idea hit me in the head. I should have thought of it when I was with her. It wasn't the first time I had thought of the right words too late. Sometimes, shaking hands at the door with my exiting parishioners at the end of services, ideas or illustrations would come to mind that would have clinched my sermon and put it over the top. In such moments I wished I could get all the worshipers back into their pews to dazzle them with my belated insights. But, alas, too late. It was not too late, however, to share my inspiration with my friend. I would do it as soon as possible.

I couldn't wait. I was back the very next day. I told her that I had been thinking about her dread of dying in the wintertime, and of her wish and prayer that she would die in the summertime. "It's silly and I know it," she said. "Maybe," I answered, "but your fear is real and we must deal with it." I pulled up closer in my chair in order to share my brilliant solution. "Look at it this way," I urged. "If God takes you in the winter, he will cover you with a blanket of white. On the other hand, if he takes you in the summer months, he will cover you with a blanket of green. All we are talking about is the color of a blanket," I said triumphantly. "So what difference does it make whether the color of the blanket is white or green?"

I leaned back, feeling quite good about myself. I felt even better when I saw my idea sink in and the muscles of her face relax from a look of concern to a smile. "Of course," she said, "that helps." It was one of those moments when I felt good about having gotten out of bed in the morning. I had done somebody some good that day. I could see it in her eyes.

Before I left, I offered a prayer about blankets, how they come in different colors and how we all have our preferences. I also told the Lord that their colors are immaterial when we close our eyes and go to sleep. I thought it was a pretty good prayer. I walked to the door. I had its handle in my hand and turned to say goodbye. I could see that she wanted to say something, so I paused. She said, "Thank you for your thoughts, but Pastor, if it's all the same to God, I'd just as soon that he covered me with a blanket of green."

A letdown! My brilliant idea went out the window before I had gone out the door. "Let's talk about it again," I said, and closed the door behind me. Driving away, I consoled myself. I thought that maybe after thinking about it some more, she would come around to my point of view.

She was moved to a rest home. That's where she died. I conducted her funeral. We went to the cemetery. There, God covered her with a blanket of . . .

White! Just like her mother. I thought of it as I stood beside her grave while I uttered the words of committal.

Before she died, it was apparent to both of us that, contrary to her many petitions, God would take her in the wintertime. She spoke of it. "It was a lovely thought," she said to me, "you with your blankets of white and green. But I know now that it will be a white one, and it's all right." She rested to catch her breath. "It's all right because, just think," she said, "I'll be home for Christmas!"

And she was. She died the day before.

I still think that my idea of the blankets was a good one. But she came up with a better thought. Home for Christmas!

It took all her thinking, and mine too, away from blankets— white or green or yellow or brown or whatever.

Liberal-
Conservative

In liberal churches there are those known as "the conservatives." In conservative churches there are those known as "the liberals." A conservative in a liberal church would probably be a liberal in a conservative church, and vice versa. The labels may vary: "traditionalist" versus "progressive," for example. Garrison Keillor writes about "dark Lutherans" and "happy Lutherans."

In any church or denomination, factions spend much energy warring with each other. The conservatives tend to be judgmental—they think everything they stand for is a matter of principle. They can be pretty hard on the preacher when he doesn't measure up. But so can their counterparts, the liberals, when they consider the pastor to be too narrow. Meanwhile, both camps may be standing within the perimeters of their confessions.

As a seminary student I preached every Sunday morning in a small Presbyterian church whose members, good Calvinists all, attended movies but were death on smoking. Evenings I often preached in a Reformed church, where the male members, good Calvinists all, smoked like chimneys but were death on movies. The morning crowd would have excommunicated me for smoking, but movies were all right. The evening crowd would have excommunicated me for going to the movies, but smoking was OK.

Older church members tend to be more cautious. Age tends towards conservatism. I remember two men in one of my churches, one of whom seemed to have avoided the narrowing views that come with the years. The other, to use a worn-out phrase, was a staunch conservative. These two, although friends and fellow members, were often in each other's hair. As their pastor, I sought to loosen up Mr. Staunch Conservative and to tighten up Mr. Liberal.

When I began as their pastor, there were a number of parties and receptions put on by the various societies in the church. One of them, called The Brotherhood, a men's Bible study group, organized a very fine reception and banquet for their new pastor and his wife. Mr. Staunch Conservative was the master of ceremonies. Sitting next to him during the dinner hour, I soon discovered his leanings. Things were getting out of hand! People were skipping evening services! Some members who had cottages were allowing their children to wade up to their knees in the lake on Sundays! He predicted a day when they would allow swimming on Sundays just like any other day of the week. (He was right.)

He said that as the master of ceremonies, it was his privilege to introduce me. This introduction, as it turned out, filled me with fearful apprehension. He said that since they were a Bible study group, it would not be out of order to ask me a test Bible question. It was not out of order to ascertain the amount of Bible knowledge their new pastor possessed. I felt a tightening in the pit of my stomach. I looked vainly around for a way to escape. I prayed that the floor would open and swallow me whole like the earth swallowed Old Testament Koran, Dathan, and Abiram. Instead, I had to sit there and look pleasant when

I knew that I would surely fail the test and be humiliated. I never did think very clearly when put on the spot. I resigned myself to my fate. I was beginning my ministry among them with three strikes against me.

"Are you ready for your test question?" asked Mr. Staunch Conservative. The party had turned into a courtroom. I felt like a man condemned.

"Jesus said, 'It is more blessed to give than to receive.' In which gospel is that statement found? In Matthew, Mark, Luke, or John?" My spirit soared through the ceiling. Hallelujah! I knew the answer before he had finished his trick question. It was a trap into which I would not fall. I tried hard not to look relieved.

I rose to my feet and assumed a professional air. I turned the tables on my inquisitor. I said I was surprised that the master of ceremonies, a leader of The Brotherhood, a Bible study group, was so uninformed on the contents of the Holy Scriptures. I said that my teaching ministry in the congregation might as well begin with him, and so I proceeded to instruct the master of ceremonies in the presence of all his colleagues. I said, "Mr. Toastmaster, we all know, as apparently you do not, that these words of Jesus are not found in the gospel of Matthew, nor in Mark, nor in Luke, nor in John. Indeed, not in any of the gospels." I said that if he would look in another book, namely the Acts of the Apostles, that he would find this verse. I offered to show it to him after the banquet.

I was "in." Everyone applauded, Mr. Staunch Conservative loudest of all. It was the beginning of a beautiful friendship.

But I digress. Mr. Staunch Conservative had a friend in the congregation who generally viewed all things from a broader perspective. These two, as I have already mentioned, were often in each other's hair. One day, being in the neighborhood, I dropped in at Mr. Liberal's place of business and found Mr. Staunch Conservative there as well. They were drinking coffee together and, as usual, having a disagreement. They saw me coming. "Good," said one of them. "Here comes the pastor. He can settle the argument."

It was too late for me to avoid what had the potential to be a ticklish situation. "We were talking about a mutual friend who dropped dead suddenly. He had just had his annual physical. The doctor pronounced him to be in excellent health. But as he was leaving the doctor's waiting room, before he was even in the hall outside the door, the Lord took him. Just like that. Here one second and gone the next!"

Mr. Staunch Conservative was doing the talking. "My liberal friend here says that's how he wants to go. Quick. In a flash. But I disagree. I pray for a deathbed. I want to linger a little at death's door so that I can gather all my children around me and have one more opportunity to witness to them and to point them all in the right direction."

I could see in Mr. Staunch Conservative's eyes that he was envisioning and even enjoying the dramatic scene he had sketched.

Mr. Liberal put in his rebuttal. "You've been telling them the way of life for years. You don't have to lie there in bed and be holy and dramatic and play on their emotions. No sirree. And you don't need any warning either. You've got one foot in heaven already. As for me, I don't need a warning either. I'm ready now. But when I go, I'd rather go with my boots on instead of with my bare feet in a bed."

Mr. Staunch Conservative turned to me. He wanted me to settle the matter (in his favor, of course). Reluctant to choose sides, I tried to be a diplomat. I changed the subject. I said that their discussion reminded me of a cartoon in the funnies called "Mutt and Jeff." Mutt said to Jeff that he wished he knew the place where he was going to die. Jeff asked "Why?" and Mutt said, "Because if I knew the place where I was going to die, I'd never go there." "So," I said, "none of us has control over the circumstances or manner of our deaths, but when the time comes, we'll all be at the spot from which God has chosen to exit us out of this world and into the next."

What I said satisfied neither of them. "You're avoiding the question, Reverend," said Mr. Liberal. "Do you agree with me or with Mr. Fussbudget here? Quick, or a lingering death? I vote for quick."

I still didn't want to get involved. "Look at it this way," I said, "which would be easier on the families you leave behind?" Alas, my question started a whole new argument.

In time, I buried both of them. Mr. Liberal did not go quick, like he wanted. Instead, his was a slow death. He wasted away. In the end, he died in his sleep.

Mr. Staunch Conservative got his wish. And yet he didn't. His children were all gathered around his deathbed when he died—just as he had wanted. But in the years following our conversation, he had developed Alzheimer's disease. When he died, he didn't know his children were there.

I still think of these two sometimes. It has been years since their deaths. Each was a loss for the church on earth. In his retirement, Mr. Staunch Conservative preached every week in a rest home. When he was old and feeble and could hardly stand, they propped him up so that he could still speak his piece for the Lord. Only when his mind began to ramble was his long-time mission terminated.

Mr. Liberal, too, was a pillar of the church. He was a faithful steward and a willing worker. When I asked both one day how they could be such good friends when they were poles apart on so many issues, they said that they counterbalanced each other and that was good.

Maybe this is why God has both types in his church. But when the conservatives go and sit in one corner and the liberals in another, neither profits from the other's wisdom, both become stubborn in their own viewpoints, and the work and witness of the church suffers.

A Very Long Stairway

My seminary professors never taught me how to throw pebbles in the middle of the night. They taught me:

Greek and Hebrew, systematic theology, and church history.

Greek and Hebrew, Christian ethics, and apologetics.

Green and Hebrew, Old Testament theology, and New Testament theology.

Greek and Hebrew, biblical theology, and pastoral psychology.

None of which helped me in throwing pebbles in the night. Not even all that Greek and Hebrew. But I threw the pebbles anyway. When you are a minister, you do what you have to do.

It was close to midnight one evening when the doorbell rang. There stood a forlorn parishioner. I asked him in. He came right to the point. "My wife won't let me in the house," he said. I called her on the telephone, but she didn't answer. So I went along with him to his house and rang the doorbell. Again, there was no answer. He pointed to their bedroom on the second floor. Can you believe it? There I stood in the dark of night throwing pebbles at the window. Like I said—when you're a minister, you do what you have to do.

Suddenly, the window was flung open wide to reveal an irate wife. It certainly was far from a Romeo and Juliet scene. "Go away, John, or I'll call the cops." She sounded like she meant it. I answered. "I'm not John, I'm your pastor." What a way to make a pastoral call! When I quickly added that John was with me, and that we had some talking to do like good Christians, she let us in. It took her all of ten minutes to come to the door. I came home in time for breakfast, having spent the night doing "patchwork" and drinking a gallon of coffee.

At the monthly pastors' union meeting, I talked to an older, wiser, and more experienced man of the cloth. I wanted some pointers on how to handle emergency marital problems. "Not my own," I added hastily. As it turned out, he was no help, even though he pontificated. "All marriages are unsuccessful," he intoned, "some are just more unsuccessful than others." He continued: "All married people fall into one of two classifications. There are those who divorce, and there are those who stick it out." I thanked him for his advice and moved to another seat. I needed to make some space between us.

Nowadays there are oodles of marriage counselors around, but in my fledgling years in the ministry there were few. But even if I could have referred John's wife to one of them, I don't think that she would have availed herself of such a service. I just hoped that I would not have to throw more pebbles at her window at night.

I thought of that older minister at the Pastor's Union meeting when another marital problem was thrown into my lap.

Another one? Were that older clergyman's words closer to the truth than I thought?

It started with a telephone call from Mrs. Mouse. She was the wife of Mr. Grouch. These were private labels that I had conferred on them, and for good reason. They were an older couple, and faithful churchgoers. From his facial expression in the pew, I gathered that the sermons I delivered were like lemons in his mouth. They were still there when I shook his hand at the door. His wife always walked a respectful three steps behind him and had no opinions but his.

I had called on Mr. Grouch several months before when he was a patient in the hospital. As we spoke, he referred to my sermon of the previous Sunday. He did so with that same facial expression, as if regurgitating another lemon. I was somewhat comforted when I noticed that he employed the same sour grimace when he criticized the care he was receiving from the nurses.

I have noticed through the years that being confined to a hospital bed often reveals a person's true nature. There are those who suffer with patience. They appreciate the smallest favors. Others, under similar circumstances, show their worst sides. Nurses could write books about what happens to human nature when it is exposed to bedpans. Mr. Grouch, spending a week in a private room, had succeeded in thoroughly alienating all the angels of mercy assigned to him. Nevertheless, they kept returning good for ill.

Each time I called, he grumbled. Mrs. Mouse didn't drive, so I offered to take Mr. Grouch home the day he was released. I found him fit to be tied. He had been overcharged $1.19. He said it was probably for the aspirin he was given that morning. I said I would adjudicate the matter. I went down to the office, paid the $1.19, and had a new bill issued minus the $1.19. "You were right," I lied, "they overcharged." I thought my kind deed might remove the lemon from his mouth. It didn't. That's when, mentally, I baptized him "Mr. Grouch."

It may be that I am overstating things a bit. After all, he did have some redeeming features. It's just that they were hard to find. The lines in his face had not fallen into pleasant places. It had been a relief not to preach to that face for a few Sundays, but after a month he was back in church. The vicissitudes of life had not altered his expression. His tag-along wife had followed him from the car and down the aisle to his accustomed pew, in which no one else dared to sit. Behind him sat John's wife—the one at whose window I hoped I would not have to throw any more pebbles. In my mind, I had a text for her—Ecclesiastes 7:16: "Be not righteous overmuch." For Mr. Grouch, who upon his return to church had a fresh lemon in his mouth, I had another—Ecclesiastes 7:17: "Be not overmuch wicked."

In contrast to her husband, Mrs. Mouse was the soft-spoken sort, a woman kindly in manner. I had never had a real conversation with her, since that was impossible in the presence of her husband. She seemed to have no opinions of her own. That's what made her telephone call one weekday morning surprising. She asked whether I could come over. She asked whether I could come right away.

Her husband worked as a groundskeeper for a very wealthy tycoon. Together Mr. Grouch and Mrs. Mouse occupied an ample apartment above a five-car garage. Inside the garage, a very long stairway led upstairs. She met me at the top of it and got right down to business. Her husband had not spoken to her for a week. He had refused to come upstairs, and at night he slept on a cot between the cars. She was being punished for something, but she didn't know what. She had gone down the long stairway several times to talk to him and to bring him food, but he acted as if she weren't there. She said she was a prisoner in her own house. She said, "Reverend, I can't drive, but unless something happens soon, I am leaving on foot and without any money."

She looked out the window and paled. Her husband had returned earlier than expected. She said, "I didn't want him to know that you were here." I said I would go down and talk to him. I descended the long stairway.

He looked surprised. I came right to the point. "Your wife asked me to come. She told me—" and I proceeded to tell him what she had told me.

"Is that so!" he thundered, with his lemon in his mouth. "Well, you can go right up there and tell her—" and he proceeded to tell me what I should tell her. I went up the long stairway and told her what he told me to tell her. When she heard what her husband told me to tell her, she got on her high horse. It was a strange sight to see a mouse on a high horse. She told me to go down and tell him that what he had told me to tell her was a complete fabrication (what she actually said was that it was a bunch of horse manure—but I changed it to "a complete fabrication" when I conveyed her message) and that she was ashamed of a husband who lied like that.

I went back down the long stairway which, by this time, had become a *very* long stairway, and found Mr. Grouch making himself a cup of coffee on a hot plate. He sat down between two expensive-looking cars and began to sip his brew. I told him what she had told me to tell him, omitting the reference to what the horse she was sitting on produced. As I listened, I began to wonder why I had found the ministry so attractive. Having denied his wife's accusation that he was a liar, he told me to go right up there and tell her—and he told me what to tell her.

I had bounded up the very long stairway the first time in youthful vigor. Now I ascended more slowly on what had become Jacob's ladder. I counted the steps. There were twenty-seven of them. Reaching the top, I delivered the message. She began to weep, suddenly stopped, and became uncharacteristically aggressive again. She told me to go down and tell that man—and she told me what to tell him. I descended the very long stairway again. Going down was easier than going up. He had finished his coffee and was pretending to be busy doing something. I told him what his wife had told me to tell him. He exploded.

By this time I could see that I wasn't getting anywhere at all. Furthermore, I was sick of playing messenger boy. Jesus said, "Blessed are the peacemakers," and I was trying. At the same time I had no desire to spend my whole day in calisthenics, ascending and descending that very long stairway. When Mr. Grouch told me to go upstairs and tell his wife another thing or two, I said, "On one condition. I will convey your sentiments, but only if you will sit on the bottom of the stairs and stay there." He grumbled, but promised to do as I asked.

I back went up the very long stairway. I told Mrs. Mouse, who wasn't so mouselike anymore, that I had a message from her husband but to hear it she must sit on the top step of the stairway. She promised and complied. Now we were getting somewhere. At least I had them in sight of each other, yet not too close, for it was indeed a very long stairway.

I took up a position halfway between them on the very long stairway, looked up and told her what her husband had told me to tell her. She found the message entirely unacceptable and told me what to tell him. Her husband heard what she told me to tell him, but waited for me to repeat it to him. Again he told me to convey his reply to his wife. I did, without moving. My tired body considered this progress. They could now hear each other, although they were still using me as a conduit.

Having moved this whole operation to stage two, I now tried for stage three. I suggested she come down a step and that he come up a step, because the long stairway made it difficult to communicate without shouting. This, I figured, was quite literally a step-by-step process. I found that both of them, having blown off a lot of steam, were becoming more pliable. Eventually we grouped together in the middle of that very long stairway. Suddenly Mrs. Mouse said that it was silly for the three of us to be sitting in the middle of the stairway, so why didn't we all go up and have some soup.

When I left, I felt that we had at least attained a truce between them, if not peace. On my way home I thought of the older minister who had said that some married people just stick it out. Mrs. Mouse almost didn't. In the end, she was glad she did. So was Mr. Grouch, although he would never say so as long as he kept that lemon in his mouth. It was hours before I came home, having done some pastoral work and gotten some exercise at the same time on that very long stairway.

Throwing pebbles at a window in the dark of night. Running up and down, climbing and descending a very long stairway which eventually seemed like Mt. Everest . . . like I said, "There are a lot of things they don't teach you in seminary." I am sure, though, that I could still climb that very long stairway with the twenty-seven steps. At the mall where I shop there is a restroom on the second floor. It can be reached by an elevator or by using the very long stairway. When I use the latter, I count.

It has twenty-seven steps.

Pinkie

When you play the game of "Open the doors and see all the people," let your pinkies remind you of children. Besides my parental home, nothing has influenced my life more—for good—than the church in which I was a pinkie. There is an old hymn, "The Church in the Wildwood," that contains the line "No spot is so dear to my childhood." I had two. Home and church were the focal points of my life.

When I first met the church of my childhood, I was baptized, being an infant of only a few weeks old. I do not remember the event. My earliest memory of my church is of sitting under a table, holding a toy and looking at a lot of feet. These were attached to about a dozen women who, together, were known as the Ladies' Aid. I also list among my earliest memories a minister who spoke interminably; the Sunday school superintendent, whose pants were too long; and Alice, my Sunday school teacher, who was so beautiful I hardly dared look at her.

I remember a callow youth of sixteen, gifted enough to play the hand-pumped organ. The man who pumped it disappeared behind it, and always emerged into view after the congregational singing, wiping his brow with a huge white handkerchief. One Sunday morning the young organist, who sat directly in the pew in front of us, fell asleep with his legs crossed during the sermon. When the sermon ended, his mother prodded him awake. Bounding into the aisle, he sprawled headlong as he came down on the leg that was asleep. Scrambling to his feet, he went down again on the leg that would not hold him. He looked like he had been stricken with the Spirit—a holy roller, surrounded by stern Calvinists.

Morning and evening services were conducted in the Dutch language. Afternoon services were held in English. I remember the consternation, if not the reason for it, when the minister unilaterally reversed this arrangement. The people were in shock. I wondered what the fuss was all about. Years later it was explained to me that if it had not been for the pastor's charisma, he would not have gotten away with it.

Those were the days of the Purple Gang in Detroit, which were as bad as the Al Capone group in Chicago. All Purple Gang members drove big Buicks. So did our pastor. One day he was shot at by a member of a rival gang. The following month he took a call to a church in Muskegon. Several church members wondered if this was a genuine acceptance of a call, or if the pastor was afraid of being shot at again. Years later I shared that story—it had become a legend—with the minister. He roared with laughter.

Eventually the church of my childhood was sold, and services were held for a time in the second-floor auditorium of a Lutheran church whose school I was attending. My cousin, who attended the same school, starred in a school play in which she had to go charging around on the auditorium steps yelling "My stars and chicken gizzards!" Our new pastor, whose walk I could imitate to perfection, was preaching from the very stage where my cousin had been yelling "My stars and chicken gizzards!" I remember thinking that it was most unseemly that our minister, while dispensing truth, had to stand on such an unhallowed spot—unhallowed by stars and chicken gizzards.

In due time, I stood with some friends my age watching the minister and elders conduct a cornerstone-laying ceremony. The day was hot. People in the neighborhood were on their porches. I wondered what they were thinking about us—a bunch of people singing a Dutch psalm. We worshiped in the basement while the superstructure was being built. When the building was completed, there were tears of joy in my parents' eyes. I remember the enormous pride that I, too, felt, sitting in our bright, new, shining church.

When we were "between" ministers, the visiting clergymen usually stayed at our house, arriving on Saturday and leaving on Monday. I recall how some of them paid attention to me and how others ignored me. On those days when we were without a minister and without a visiting clergyman, the leading elder, a man with a heavy Dutch accent, would read a sermon. Such services were generally awkward and dull. Even so, congregational attendance never lagged.

I remember joy, verging on ecstasy, when it was announced that a pastor-designate had accepted our call. To my delight, he turned out to be a great animal lover. In no time he was a visitor at our house where, in the middle of a big city, my father had sixty-four rabbits, homing pigeons, chickens, pheasants, an outdoor pool with giant goldfish, and—inside— canaries and tropical fish. Our pastor also turned out to be a very good catechism teacher. I remember my catechism book, *First Book of Doctrine* by Hylkema and Tuuk, all rolled up in the back pocket of my corduroy pants. Hylkema, as it turned out, would serve as our church's pastor at a later date.

The pastor we had, the one who taught catechism so well, was a man who was "strong"—as they said—on Christian education. With his leadership and inspiration, and despite the depths of the Depression the country was in, a Christian school was built for grades 1-8. A call was extended to an educator with an excellent reputation. He accepted and became our first principal. A young woman was engaged to teach the first four grades. It was a time when many men in the church were unemployed. There were occasions when the teachers and the pastor couldn't be paid. Yet these, the poorest days of the church of my childhood, were also in many ways its richest days. There was a strong sense of belonging to each other. Mutual help gave all a sense of security. Our church was our spiritual home. There were no other churches of our denomination in the big city of Detroit. We were family.

As in all families, quarrels occasionally broke out. Many men in the church were self-made, strong individualists, manifesting ethnic stiff-neckedness. There were earth-shaking issues, such as how we should observe the Sabbath, whether women could wear bobbed hair, and whether we should use the common cup or individual cups for the sacrament of communion.

I remember coming to church one Sunday in our brand-new Hupmobile. After the service my father and a friend, a fellow elder, stood facing each other, the hood of our brand-new Hupmobile between them. They were differing on the subject of the common versus the individual cup. My anxious mother was sitting in the front seat of the car, and we children were in the back seat. My father's friend, who felt so strongly for the common cup, began using the hood of our brand-new Hupmobile as a pulpit, pounding on it so hard that he put a dent in it. On the way home, Mother chastised Father. She said that religious arguments (my father said they were having a "discussion") were wrong when they resulted in damaged cars. That evening after church my father's friend and his wife were at our house for cake and coffee.

Our church, with its high walls of separation from the world, was nevertheless an outreaching community. Evangelistic services were conducted every Sunday afternoon at a nearby Marine hospital on the banks of the Detroit River. Street-corner meetings were held weekly in the inner city at two different locations. Many young people came to help with the singing. One of our leaders, a rather flamboyant fellow, would sometimes literally stand on his head to draw a crowd.

Our church was our recreational center (where else could you find a church that had a picnic every week?). With school and catechism and Sunday school, it was also our educational center. We had our own band and orchestra, so it was also our musical center. Considering our many societies, it was also our social center. And with those interminable programs that we put on twice a year, with every society contributing something to the program (a solo, a poem, a duet, a recitation, etc.), it was also our cultural center. The first piano solo I ever played, with one finger, was for the Christmas program. "O Little Town of Bethlehem."

And so, Sundays—services and Marine hospital. Mondays—orchestra practice. Tuesdays—Boys' Society. Wednesdays—catechism classes. Thursdays—street-corner meetings. And Saturdays—picnics on Belle Isle.

When I was fifteen, I began practicing on the organ for playing the psalms for the afternoon Dutch services. And what an organ it was! A committee of five Hollanders, whose combined knowledge of organs you could put in a thimble, traveled to Toledo, Ohio, where they bought a bargain (what else?)—a Wurlitzer theater organ, which they rescued from its worldly use. It arrived, complete with cow bells. There were a few more such irreverent stops, which we removed. And so we had, if not exactly a church organ, an organ nonetheless.

We didn't dedicate it. Such services of dedication were unknown to us. But we surely used it. The callow youth with the sleeping leg, having matured, played with zest and fury. An assistant, a woman, played more quietly. And everybody sang. Singing was something we did well. We had a "singing school," later called the "choir," which could perform on occasional Sundays, but only after the benediction or before the invocation. Choirs had no proper place in the official liturgy as constructed by the Synod, the broadest assembly of our denomination.

I remember one of my father's business associates, a sometime Presbyterian, who accepted an invitation to visit one of our services. He came on Sunday evening. He couldn't believe the attendance. How did we fill the church on a Sunday evening? He couldn't believe the presence of whole families; children, young people, even babies. And he couldn't believe the singing!

The Rev. George Hylkema came, the man whose book lived, rolled up, in my hip pocket. I discovered with amazement that he was not only a preacher but also a ham-radio operator. Not only that, but he knew all about cars. One day he fixed our Model T so that it would run. We had bought it, a friend and I, for five dollars. What a man!

The church of my childhood was also the church where I met and married Anne, my wife. I had accompanied her singing so often we decided to make our association permanent. We were married during a Sunday evening service. Together we owe a great debt to an earlier generation of sterling men and women who built the church of our childhood, comprised its congregation, and gave it the character it had. I can think of at least seven sons of that church who went into the ministry and of many, many other members who took a Christian heritage, largely bestowed by our church, with them into all the world and all walks of life.

On Sunday mornings as I wend my way to church, I often see children playing in the streets. They are not going to church. They know nothing of its fellowship and the saving gospel it proclaims. I feel sorry for them. When I think more deeply, I weep for them. My parents gave me many things. But the best gift they ever gave me, besides a Christian home, was the gift of church. They didn't send me. They took me.

When you play the game "Open the doors and see all the people," let your pinkies remind you of the children. Once, I was one of them. As the years go by, may there be many, many more pinkies everywhere.

The Cucumber Lady

All work and no play makes Johnny a dull boy. Too much work also makes a preacher less than sharp. Wise Solomon didn't say this. Nevertheless, it is worthy of his signature. To paraphrase him, we might say that for everything there is a season: a time to work and a time to play (see Ecclesiastes 3). Ministers should not be workaholics. Many, wisely, take Mondays off. They need to rest from the day of rest. Those with children do well to take Saturdays off, lest their "P.K.'s" (preacher's kids) get short-changed.

Besides taking time off for family, every minister should have a hobby. One of the best is gardening. That's what one of my seminary professors said. It was his opinion that getting your fingers into God's good earth to help things grow was therapeutic. He said this was especially therapeutic for those who spend great amounts of time sitting indoors behind desks. The professor said that gardening had made him a better pastor and preacher all around. I sat up and took note, for the professor was, indeed, a very good pastor and preacher all around.

I wanted to be a good pastor and preacher all around too. But, alas, I had grown up in the confines of a big city, and I had little gardening experience. As a child, I had tried planting some radish seeds a few times in our meager yard, but nothing ever came of them. However, when I learned in seminary that gardening would serve me well, both personally and professionally, and make me a better pastor and preacher all around, I resolved that I would develop a green thumb someday.

It took me a while to get going. I never really acted on my resolution until my third charge. This is because I believed that weeding and uprooting dandelions, as I did while serving my first two churches, would fit the bill. But I found neither of these exercises therapeutic. Quite the contrary. They made me mad at Adam, who was the cause of weeds and dandelions. Pulling them up did nothing at all for me, neither personally nor professionally. If anything, these exercises made me a worse pastor and preacher all around. It didn't occur to me until I reached my third charge that what I had been doing was the exact opposite of gardening. Instead of growing things, I had been uprooting and destroying them.

I saw my opportunity. After settling down to serve my third church, I talked to a member who had a great deal of land outside the city. He had orchards too. I asked him if he could rent me an acre of ground. He asked what I wanted to rent an acre for. I said I wanted to have a garden. He rolled his eyes and asked whether I thought an acre would be enough. Having no idea how big an acre was, the thought crossed my mind to ask for two. He invited me to come out to his place at my convenience so we could talk it over. That week I drove out to his place. He showed me an acre. "That's an acre?" I exclaimed.

He chuckled.

It was embarrassing. Compared to him, I was, supposedly, the man of education. But he knew what an acre was and I didn't.

I backpedaled. I said that, really, I didn't even need half an acre. Or a quarter, or an eighth. I just wanted a little corner of his land for a garden. He was gracious. He said, "Take as much of it as you want."

I had already decided what it was that I would plant. Certainly not radishes. They never came up, as I remembered. It was cucumbers I wanted. I have always liked cucumbers. Growing up, I ate them raw with a little salt. When my mother prepared and served them, I always took more than my share and finished off what was left. I had also discovered the delights of cucumber sandwiches at numerous finger-food affairs.

Preparing the ground was more work than I cared for. I wondered how all that back-breaking labor could possibly make me a better pastor and preacher all around. I planted a few beans, a few carrots, and a few tomatoes. I had grown them from seed in my study window. I preached to them while practicing my sermons, and I developed an affection for them. Then I planted them, reluctant to part with them. I told them that they were now on their own. The next week, when I returned, they were gone. "Oh boy!" I thought, remembering the disappearing radishes of long ago.

I decided that I would like to have three or four dozen cucumbers, so I planted about six dozen, figuring that there might be some loss from weather or other reasons. To my utter amazement and delight, they appeared in due time. So did the beans and the carrots. What a miracle! I stood there looking at them and having the same feelings I had when I first became a father. (Not quite the *same* feelings, perhaps, but close.)

I was already beginning to feel like a better pastor and preacher all around. These were my plants. I had started them, and I now had the responsibility of caring for them and helping them to grow. I was sorry that I could only manage to come once a week. My garden wasn't exactly next door. It was, in fact, on the other side of town. But even when I wasn't there, I thought of my garden frequently. And when I came, I cultivated my plants lovingly. The professor had been right: "Get your fingers into mother Earth. Grow stuff. It will do things for you personally and professionally, and make you a better pastor and preacher all around."

The rains came and the sun shone. People said it was a great summer for gardening. My beans and my carrots were doing well, but my cucumbers were getting out of control. I had expected that each plant would grow up true and tall and present me with a cucumber. Instead, all of them shot out tentacles, like octopi, in all directions, crawling all over my garden and beyond. No, not like octopi. More like giant squids. I wondered whether I should cut those creepers off to conserve the plants' energy for growing taller. Somebody told me that you had to destroy those little growths on tomato plants that grew out of the crux between the main stem and the branches. Maybe my cucumber plants had to be trimmed too. But no, I was told. To paraphrase an old song, my cucumbers were doing what came naturally.

And so, multiple tentacles from six dozen plants grew longer each week while they meandered all over my garden. They showed little regard for what was supposed to be bean and carrot territory. They were definitely out of control and threatening to cover the whole earth. All I could do was observe helplessly.

I noticed that each tentacle produced a bud every twelve inches or so, and that each bud produced what looked like a pickle. Were these to become my cucumbers? Indeed! The miracle continued to unfold before my eyes. I planted more cucumbers, albeit outside the perimeters of my garden.

I began to wonder, and then to worry, about the number cucumbers I would harvest. Far more than I had planned. After all, I was in the preacher business, not the cucumber business. The summer continued to be favorable for bumper crops everywhere. The farmers were ecstatic. But I was beginning to wonder whether I had perhaps overreached myself.

I hauled my cucumbers home in bushel baskets. I shared them with family and friends. I left them, anonymously, on the back porches of strangers, like a reverse thief in the night. I had them for breakfast, lunch, and dinner. I made pastoral calls, leaving a trail of cucumbers behind. It gave me an idea. Why not take my cucumbers to church with me? Place them in bushel baskets in the narthex with a sign saying, "Free. Take one." I even considered altering our church's Saturday ad in the paper, using my cucumbers as a missionary tool. "Come to church and get a free cucumber."

The following Sunday I came to church early. I always came early. (I would have beat the janitor to church, except that he lived in an upstairs apartment in the parish house.) Arriving early was an idiosyncrasy of mine. Before the service began, I always needed to double-check everything, including whether or not all the hymnbooks were in their places, right side up. A psychiatrist friend said I did this out of a feeling of insecurity.

The second person to arrive was always the widow lady who lived on "the other side of the tracks." She was a fine person with a perpetual look of surprise on her face. It was her natural expression. She was in her sixties. Her figure was thin, angular, and completely devoid of any feminine contours. She walked with a mannish gait, crossing the railroad tracks and leaving behind the deteriorating part of town where she lived in a spare upstairs apartment. Her relatives constantly urged her to move. But she had lived there for forty years with her late husband and wouldn't think of living anywhere else. I had urged her often to allow the transportation committee of the church to arrange to pick her up and drive her home. I felt that the railroad area presented some danger for a woman walking alone, but she said she could take care of herself. Also, she needed the exercise.

Being the first two arrivals each Sunday morning, we always engaged in some small talk and thus became good friends. I liked her, and the feeling was mutual. Exchanging pleasantries on a weekly basis, I got to know her very well. "The salt of the earth," I thought.

On the morning I arrived with my load of cucumbers, she found me arranging them in the narthex, a full bushel at each end, with the "free" sign atop each one. "What's this?" she inquired, pointing to my crop. I answered playfully, "These are cucumbers, as anyone can plainly see." "I know cucumbers," she said, "but what are they doing here?" I explained my overabundance to her and said that I was giving them away. "Can I have one?" she asked, and I answered in the affirmative. "In fact," I added, "take two." She took four of the smaller ones and walked into the sanctuary to her accustomed place—the second row, directly in front of the pulpit.

Most people come to church early in order to get the back seats. Strange, when you consider that most people arrive early at programs and concerts to get the *front* seats. I know of a church in another city where the back pew is filled an hour and a half before the service begins. The tradition began with two ladies who were always practicing one-upmanship on each other. Beating each other to church was a high priority. Their rivalry did not seem to affect their friendship. Indeed, they were extra nice to each other. At the same time, the whole week was spoiled for the one who arrived second. This race had been going on, I was told, for quite a few years, during which time others had also gotten into the act. Considering that the morning service began at 9:30 a.m., these people were early risers indeed.

My friend with the cucumbers was not a back-seater. She was the first one to church and could have had her choice of seats in the back pew. Instead, she always hiked down the aisle to the front. I watched her, carrying her four cucumbers, then turned and went to my study.

It was during the sermon that I noticed something different about her. She was sitting in her usual ramrod position. With her eyebrows lifted in perpetual surprise, she was listening intently, as was her custom. Still, there was something different about her and I wondered what it was.

The human mind is a wonderful creation. It can do more than one thing at a time. Some people, as they say, can walk and chew gum at the same time. Some people can be listening to a sermon and be thinking of something else, all in the same moment. Some preachers can even do that while preaching. They can set their mouths on "automatic," continuing the message, while at the same time wondering whether the fish will be biting on Monday. Sometimes preachers can preach while thinking about something else while, at the same time, the congregation is listening but is also thinking about something else. But this is a dangerous thing to do. The mind that wanders from itself can get things confused—like the preacher who was preaching on the subject of "patience." He was going to say "pursue the spirit of patience," but his mind was on double-think, and so, in stentorian tones, he admonished his startled congregation to "pursue the spirit of perch."

Stealing another glance at my friend with the four cucumbers in the second pew, my mind went into double-think. I was preaching a catechism sermon on cucumber Sunday, while simultaneously wondering what was different about my fellow early bird. Suddenly, I realized what it was. I faltered. I lost my train of thought momentarily, but quickly recovered.

What caused my brief lapse was the discovery that my friend, who was built straight up and down, front and back, had developed a figure. Seeing some curves on her front, it came to me where her four cucumbers were. She had stashed them in strategic places under her blouse. I was aware of how some women enhanced their figures. But with cucumbers? When I shook hands with her after the service at the door, I, too, was wearing, with lifted eyebrows, an expression of surprise.

After the service, and when all had left, I discovered that my bushel baskets were empty. It made me feel good to know that a lot of people had gotten something out of the service that morning—if not from the sermon, then from one of my bushel baskets. I found a nickel in one of the empty bushels. I gave it to the deacons who were counting the money in the deacons' room.

A year later I no longer had my early bird friend to talk with before morning services. She had died. One Sunday morning, crossing the railroad tracks, she was knocked down by two young hoodlums who stole her purse. When I found her in the hospital, she was disoriented. She never recovered. Sad. Today, when I shop in the vegetable section of the supermarket, I see all the cucumbers and think of my cucumber lady. That's what I call her now whenever I think of her. We had some good talks together. Though my garden was a little out of control, my cucumber lady surely made me, both personally and professionally, a better pastor and preacher.

All around.

Three Bucks

This is a church. This is a steeple. Open the doors, and see some people getting married. Some people go to church only three times in their lives: for their baptisms, their weddings, and their funerals. Or, as it is said, when they get "hatched, matched, and dispatched."

There are those who prefer traditional ceremonies. Too bad some of them run into hitches—like groomsmen dropping rings. It happens. Sometimes members of wedding parties insist on interrupting the proceedings by fainting. It happens. They crumple and fold. I remember an exception: a very tall bridesmaid who went rigid and came down like a tree. Timber! And I remember a groom of long ago. He and his bride were kneeling while the soloist was singing the Lord's Prayer. I felt a tug on my robe. Opening my eyes I saw the bride, still kneeling, but with a distressed look in her eyes. She directed my attention to her man. He was breathing heavily and perspiring profusely. He was also beginning to list to port. He was, indeed, about to enter the world where people go when they faint. The bride propped him up on one side and I on the other. I thought the Lord's Prayer would never end. "For thine is the kingdom, and the power, and (at this point the groom decided to tune in again to his own wedding) the glory. Amen."

There are those who do not want to get hitched in the traditional manner. They want to be married barefoot, underwater, or while skydiving. The skydiving ceremonies are, of necessity, brief and to the point.

There are people who write their own wedding formalities and, sometimes, their own music. I remember a groom who insisted on writing the music and being the soloist as well. He composed a repetitious wedding song—a lengthy lyric with just three little words. We were in a small chapel, standing together at close quarters. He sang, "I love you" with wide-sweeping gestures—all the while looking only at me. I attempted to redirect his gaze by turning slightly away from him and looking fixedly at his bride, but he never took the hint.

I decline requests to officiate underwater, while skydiving, or even barefoot. I do bend a bit when the requests are for garden weddings. I forewarn the principals, however, that garden weddings are usually crashed by an uninvited fly or two. My prophesies are generally fulfilled. If not by flies, then by bees. If not by bees, then by wasps. I remember one very religious wasp who sat on my Bible while the vows were being repeated after me. The bride said, "I take thee . . . "—but that's as far as she got. There was a disconcerting disruption of the procedure as the wasp suddenly felt attracted to her beauty. It took a few minutes for her to regain her composure while the groom manfully fought off her attacker.

I remember a wedding I conducted on Lake Michigan's Beaver Island. I took advantage of the opportunity to visit a place that had once been the kingdom of James Jesse Strang. He was the Mormon elder who, when Joseph Smith died, received a vision to lead the people northward from Nauvoo, Illinois. Unfortunately, Brigham Young received a vision at the same time to lead the people westward. While the majority went west with Young, a much smaller number followed Strang to Beaver Island, a piece of land seven miles wide and fourteen miles long. It was there, at the water's edge, that I was to tie a knot between two people, at the very spot where they had first met.

The music was furnished by a friend who accompanied himself on the guitar. Alas, the weather on that designated Saturday afternoon did not cooperate. There were strong winds and turbulent waters. The strumming of the musician was barely audible. Nevertheless, the bride emerged on cue from a boat house on the arm of her father.

Now, there are not a few snakes on Beaver Island. With no warning, one of these reptiles decided to augment the meager attendance, taking up a position on the bridal path. Seeing both snake and bride, I thought of Eve in the garden. An attendant removed the unwelcome visitor, the wedding party moved into position, and I shouted at them over wind and water, asking them both if they would take each other to have and to hold. If I had asked them to promise to murder their grandmothers, it would not have made any difference, because the wind had suddenly begun to howl. I hastily pronounced the couple husband and wife. As I raised my arms in benediction, I could have called them "Bonny and Clyde" for all the difference it would have made. After the ceremony the wind swept us indoors, where the bride's mother told one and all that "it was a lovely wedding all the same."

The day of the true wedding sermon has passed. That's good. They were often too long, and aimed at bored, captive guests and heedless brides and grooms. (I prefer to speak at funerals, because people are more inclined to listen.) At weddings, brief meditations have a way of hitting the mark, provided they are in good taste. I recall one that was in bad taste in more ways than one. The minister, having pronounced the young couple husband and wife, admonished them to minister always to one another's needs. He used an illustration involving a hippopotamus that opens its big mouth to allow a little bird to pick its teeth. Sort of like a hygienist. "Mutual benefit," he said. "The hippo gets its teeth cleaned, and the bird gets something to eat." I would not have been surprised if, at that point, the beautiful bride and the handsome groom had walked out on their own wedding.

The matter of the wedding fee is always a sensitive one. Abraham Lincoln often told a story of a man and his veiled bride. The man paid the preacher a dollar so that he and his intended could "get hitched." After the ceremony the preacher lifted the veil, took a look, and gave the man seventy-five cents back.

"How much do you charge?" is a question that must be deftly handled. Some of my colleagues will not accept an honorarium if the people are members of the church. They refuse any remuneration on the grounds that they are salaried, and officiating at weddings is part of their job description. I suspect, however, that the number of these selfless pastors is few.

I am reminded of a Christian Reformed minister who was asked by a woman from the neighborhood to officiate at the funeral of her cat. He told her that he didn't do cats, but, trying to be helpful, he suggested that she go to the Episcopal church down the street where, he explained, they held annual services for the blessing of animals. She thanked him for the suggestion. Upon leaving his study, she turned at the door to ask whether he could suggest an appropriate honorarium for such a service. "Do you think that five hundred dollars would be sufficient?" she asked. The Christian Reformed minister replied, "My dear lady, you didn't tell me that your cat was a Christian Reformed cat!"

Wedding fees, in my book, should be on a sliding scale. Nothing for those who can't afford it, and something for those who can. I regret that so many weddings have become showy performances, fashion shows, and dress parades. But if people are going to blow a small fortune on such ceremonies, the preacher might just as well get in on the largesse.

I remember one such affair. No expense had been spared. The gowns! The flowers! The reception! The dinner in prestigious surroundings! I had done my part and was circulating among the guests. The groom, champagne glass in hand, called to me in a loud voice. "Rev.," he said, all eyes and ears turning his way, "I forgot to pay you." He indicated that I should follow him. I did so with embarrassment, feeling eyes on my back.

We stood in a corner, facing a wall. He took out his wallet. I could see lots of bills of various denominations. Hundreds. Fifties. Twenties. Ones. I was about to be paid. He lifted a dollar bill halfway out, then another, then another, then another which, however, he tucked back in, and gave me three bucks. "Thanks for tying the knot," he said—again in a loud voice. I said, "Thank you, thank you very much!"

Three whole dollars! I admit to having a wicked streak in me. Taking the three dollars, the streak came to the surface. I thanked him again as I said "Wow" and pressed his hand. "Oh," he said, "it's nothing." I thought, "You can say *that* again," but resisted the urge to say this aloud as he shrugged his shoulders and rejoined his friends.

Sometimes I am subject to laughing jags. My family can attest to that. I get going and can't stop. My sides begin to ache. As

I drove home, reviewing the ceremony, the plushness of the arrangements, and my three dollars, I saw the humor of it all. Four sessions of premarital counseling, a wedding rehearsal, the wedding itself, my gift of a Bible, getting my suit cleaned and pressed, etc., and all for three dollars! As I waited for a light to change at a busy corner, while laughing my head off, I noticed the driver in an adjoining car giving me a look. Seeing me all alone in my giddiness, he probably thought I was listening to some comedian on the radio.

The next morning I was in my study in church. Someone down on his luck came to the church door for a handout. We had a policy. No money. Too many simply used it to buy cheap wine. But we did give out vouchers for meals at a nearby restaurant. The man looked honest to me. That's why, besides the voucher, I also gave him the three dollars that I had received the night before from a groom who was, perhaps at that moment, flying to Hawaii with his bride.

"Three dollars," the man exclaimed. "Wow," he added—the same word I had uttered the night before in an entirely different context. And with an entirely different meaning. The man thanked me and thanked me again. As it turned out, we became friends. He started coming to church.

Some time later he told me how providential it was that he had received three dollars from me just at a time when he needed them.

Three bucks!

"It's nothing," said the groom.

"It was a lot," said the man who had been in need.

What is nothing to one is something to another.

The Visitor

Most churches welcome visitors. In vacation areas visitors sometimes outnumber the members. In more remote and rural areas visitors are few and far between. Some visitors are shoppers who come to size up the church and the minister. Others are floaters who take their religion cafeteria-style. There can be keen competition between congregations as they seek to outdo each other in being visitor-friendly.

Having been a visitor myself scores of times, I can attest to the fact that at some churches there is an overwhelming spirit of hospitality. At others this spirit is non-existent, and at still others there is a definite anti-visitor tone. Fortunately, the latter two are the exceptions.

I remember attending a service years ago in a large city where I lived for a time. I signed the guest book and found a member of the outreach committee on my doorstep the same day. Also outstanding in my memory book is a Lutheran church in another city. The pastor met me at the door, and I could sense that his welcome greeting was heartily genuine. Noticing that communion would be served, and that some Lutheran churches practiced an exclusive for-members-only communion, I asked if it was permissible for me to partake. I have never forgotten his answer. He said, "It is the Lord's table. You must ask *him.*" I don't think I could locate that church today, but it and its pastor still occupy a warm place in my heart.

On a sabbatical in Richmond, Virginia, my wife and I and our four children attended a Presbyterian church in the neighborhood where we had taken up residence. The second Sunday we had callers. Two elders—both were in their eighties. One was a retired physician and the other a retired minister who had spent more than forty years on the African mission field. I wondered how our children would react to these oldsters. In such visits the children are often overlooked. These men took a real interest in our two sons and two daughters. When one of the two men preached the sermon on Thanksgiving Day, our children listened intently, because they considered him their friend. They remember him to this day.

In Cambridge, England, where we spent another sabbatical, two matronly women called on us, both dressed in heavy tweeds and both on bicycles. One of them invited us to her house after services the following Sunday to enjoy a glass of sherry. I said, "Back home, it's coffee after church."

All of these experiences remind me of the book of Proverbs, which tells us to be "given to hospitality." They also remind me of my parental home. Strangers in church generally ended up at our house. For coffee.

My last charge—the LaGrave Avenue Christian Reformed Church of Grand Rapids, Michigan, was situated directly across the street from a beer store. I invited the proprietor to visit a service. To my surprise, he came one Sunday morning while his daughter minded the store. He never came again, but we remained friends. He always remembered the invitation with appreciation. He said no one had ever invited him before. He had always feared the possibility of a petition from us to the city council to close him down because of his proximity to the church. One winter, while vacationing in Florida, we attended services in a beautiful church over-looking the Atlantic Ocean. Its name was "Bethesda by the Sea." I was introduced to the pastor as a minister from Michigan. He asked the name of my church. I told the pastor of "Bethesda by the Sea" that I was the pastor of "LaGrave by the Beer Store."

Next door to the beer store there was a large taxicab garage, complete with a dispatcher who was in constant touch with the cab drivers as they made their way around town. For some reason his orders were sometimes picked up by our public address system. It was a very disruptive situation. The dispatcher's voice would break into our services at the oddest moments. One elderly member said it was the work of the devil. A moment of near hilarity arrived one Sunday morning as I was preaching on the son who said to his father, "'I go, sir', but he went not" (Matt. 21:30). No sooner had I said the words than the voice of the dispatcher was heard coming out of our loudspeaker, ordering a driver to go to some corner in town to pick up a fare. Afterwards I said to the elderly member that the interruption was not the work of the devil, because the devil has no sense of humor.

Our complaints to the taxicab company bore fruit. A radio tower that reached higher than our steeple was installed atop their building. I watched a part of the operation, quite fascinated with the expertise of the man doing the job. I met him and expressed my admiration. I invited him in for a cup of coffee. It turned out that he was moonlighting. He was really a police officer. A lieutenant. Lieutenant Pierce. I found out later that he was also a WWII hero, having been awarded the Congressional Medal of Honor.

I invited him to attend one of our services. He came. He had a commanding appearance that was hard to miss. When I shook hands with him at the door after the service, he said, "I notice that some of your ceiling lights are burned out." I had hoped for some favorable comment on our sanctuary, or on our choir, or even on my sermon. But, instead, it appeared that he was more interested, if not in things on high, in things up high. "Yes," I said, "the church is still quite new, and we haven't figured out a way yet to reach those ceiling lights." He said, "Leave it to me."

He called the following day to say that he had paved the way. He had spoken with some firemen in the fire station down the street and asked them to change our burned-out lights. I asked what that would cost. He said that the men would do it as a favor. He added, "Just give them each a beer." I wondered whether this was on the up-and-up and said so. "What if they are needed for a fire?" I asked. He answered, "Those who said they would help will do so when they are off duty." "What about the equipment they will use—is it city property?" I asked. "That's no problem," he said. I didn't consider his answer very enlightening. I had another thought. "I don't think it is proper," I said, "for a church to give out a case of beer. How about Bibles?" The lieutenant said, "Don't give them anything. Just say 'Thank you.'"

I found this interchange less than satisfying. I thanked the lieutenant and said that I, or someone else, would get back to him. I called the chairman of the facilities committee and told him about the deal. I said, "You handle it." Why did I feel a little like Pilate washing his hands?

A week or so later I found several firemen in our sanctuary with extension ladders and ropes. They were changing burned-out light bulbs. I thanked them. A few days later I walked past the open doors of the fire station down the street on my way to a nearby hospital. I thanked the men again. They smiled. One of them said, "Thanks for the beer."

The beer!?

The lieutenant was back in church again. A visitor. I shook his hand at the door. He observed that all the ceiling lights were working. "Looks better," he said. I invited him to come back again. His answer was an invitation. "I've visited you," he said. "Now you visit me."

The police station was an old building completely lacking in charm. It had been marked for razing and replacement in the near future. I was fascinated by the behind-the-scenes activities, but I felt that I was out of my element. The lieutenant made small talk, then he suddenly sprang an idea on me. I had been asking about his work and experiences, and why he had the reputation of being so fearless. He said, "Why don't you ride with me in the patrol car for a night?" It was more a statement than a question. I said that it would be great, even though I had some reservations about the idea. It really wasn't my cup of tea.

I had a part-time assistant at the time, a seminary student. He was "gung-ho," as they say, for the idea when I mentioned it to him. And so it was that, on a designated night, I said a fond farewell to my wife and, together with my seminary student, showed up at the station for a night ride with the lieutenant. My sermons for the following Sunday were prepared—just in case I lived long enough to preach them. We were told that we would be in a scout car from 11 p.m. to 7 a.m.

It was a quiet night. Nothing much happened. We roamed all over town. There was an accident, a fire, a speeder. The lieutenant kept up a running conversation, except when he stepped on it and turned the siren on to respond to a directive by radio. It was a secure feeling to go flying through town far in excess of the speed limit and know that we couldn't get a ticket.

Around 2 a.m. we stopped at an all-night greasy spoon for a cup of coffee. There were a few others there, nursing coffee cups. The banter was light and pleasant. The lieutenant introduced me as his supervisor, even though I didn't look the part, and I introduced my assistant as mine. Refreshed, we were off again. My assistant was getting sleepy, and he had exams coming up. Since the night was mostly spent and nothing big was happening, he suggested that we drop him off when we came into his neighborhood. I had the same inclination but, on second thought, decided to stick it out till 7 a.m.

No sooner had we dropped off the seminary student at his home than we received instructions to proceed, pell-mell, to an all-night store a few blocks from my church where a robbery had just taken place. We must have hit sixty, the siren wailing. I was wishing that the lieutenant would go a little slower so we would be a little late. I had no desire to be in the middle of a "situation." But it was obvious that my lieutenant, honored for bravery in WWII, and with a Congressional Medal of Honor, was born for this sort of thing.

We arrived on the scene in no time flat. My leader jumped out of the scout car and shouted an order at me: "Stick behind me!" We burst into the store. The man behind the counter was surprisingly calm. No doubt he had experienced a robbery or two before. He said, "The guy headed for Division Avenue." That's all I heard. The lieutenant whirled, went out and headed for Division Avenue on foot. I followed orders. I stuck behind him.

A light snow had fallen. He followed a set of footprints far enough apart to indicate that they had been made by someone who was running. They led into an alley. What in the world was I doing in that alley at 4:30 in the morning and in that part of town? I should have had my head examined. The footsteps led into a yard, around a house, and up its front porch steps. The lieutenant, with the instinct of a hound, bounded up the steps of the large two-story dwelling. There were no lights on inside. I saw no reason for disturbing the peace of those who were slumbering there. But my leader was of a different persuasion. "Open up!" he yelled, as he banged on the door and then—imagine—kicked it open. His pistol, at the ready, was in front of him and I was behind him. Didn't he need a search warrant or something? We were inside. He bellowed for lights. To my amazement lights went on and there, before us, stood about twenty people, fully clothed. "Where is he?" shouted the lieutenant. At the same time, still following his instinct, he flew up the stairs as he turned to me and shouted, "Detective, you're in charge!"

Who? *Me?* There I stood, minus my protector, in a roomful of strangers. Their looks were sullen. There was, for me, an unbearable silence. I felt I had to say something. I said, "I hear we've got a little more snow coming our way today."

What a dumb thing to say! What a stupid remark to make to a roomful of sullen strangers at 4:30 in the morning! But what were they all doing there anyway, and why wasn't there any furniture?

Mercifully, I was in charge for less than a minute. Backup officers came flying through the door. At the same time, my lieutenant friend came downstairs. He had found the culprit in a closet. He led him into the room handcuffed. The backup officers took over, and we left.

Before 7 a.m. we were in the police station. I stayed with the lieutenant while he made his full report. I watched the thief being booked. Someone from the press was hanging around. He took notes. I said, "Good night," or rather, "Good morning," to the lieutenant and some others, went home, and tumbled into bed.

I woke up around three in the afternoon. The paper came. The headline said, "Local clergyman assists in arrest." Actually, all I had done was hide behind the lieutenant as best I could. Oh yes, and I had remarked about the weather to a roomful of strange characters. A mile or so away, my seminary student also woke up, opened his paper, read the headline, and slammed the paper on the floor in disgust. He had missed the action altogether.

The following Sunday I was something of a hero in church. Youngsters sized me up with new eyes. As I sat in the pulpit chair, I looked up at the ceiling and thought of a lieutenant who had brought more light into our sanctuary and who had made me more conscious of those brave people who patrol our streets at night so that we can sleep in peace.

I had invited and followed up on a visitor to our church and got more than I bargained for. The lieutenant never did come back. He had his own church. But we stayed in touch. And, ever after, I have made it a point to pray for our police and firefighters, our mayors and commissioners, our judges, our social workers, and all those who are there in God's providence, and without whom our cities would be uninhabitable.

Tom, Dick, and Harry

People live longer these days, and, generally, women live longer than men. In consequence, many a church can count more widows than widowers on its membership roll. The so-called "weaker sex" is, in fact, the stronger sex. What is more, women cope better with old age and loneliness. Old men, if they live alone, don't take care of themselves as well as their counterparts do. There are, of course, exceptions.

My pastoral record book lists a number of marriages that I performed between widows and widowers—second marriages for both parties. None of them ever ended in divorce. For these couples, companionship lifted their loneliness, bringing happiness and a new lease on life.

Most, however, do not reenter the marital state in old age. And some, of course, reach the evening of life having lived all their days in singleness. There was Dick, for example, who had never married. But there was also Tom who had, and Harry who had twice walked down the aisle. These were not their real names. The first was "Dick" because his middle name was Dick. The second was "Tom" for me because that was his nickname. The third I called "Harry," but not to his face. I really thought of him as "Hairy" because he had the most beautiful head of white hair I have ever seen on an old man.

These three were octogenarians and members of my flock. All three lived alone. In each case their situations were not ideal. As their pastor I was concerned with their temporal as well as their eternal well-being. I urged all three to take the necessary steps, with the church's help, to enter a retirement home. All three arrived at such places eventually—but in very different ways.

Tom

Tom was a widower. He had no children. Despite a limited education he was a self-taught theologian. He carried commentaries with him to the meetings of The Brotherhood, a thriving men's society in the church, where heavy doctrinal discussions took place amid clouds of cigar smoke. Tom was also a much-better-than-average chess player; he attended the weekly meetings of the city chess club, which met a few blocks from our church in the downtown YMCA.

Tom was a man of very limited means. Despite a physical handicap, he was also a man of self-confidence and pride. He told me one day in confidence that it bothered him that he could not hold up his end in church, financially speaking. That was the reason that he was always looking for a way to make "a bundle." It was one of his expressions. He assured me that if he ever did make "a bundle," he would give it all to the church. I believed him.

It was the time of "The $64,000 Question," a program on television, which was soon superseded by a $100,000 quiz show. Tom was hooked on these and other contests. Watching a contestant failing to answer a question in the "Bible" category, Tom grew excited. He had known the correct answer.

If only he had stood in the place of the person who failed, he could have made "a bundle" and given it to the church.

One day he phoned to inform me that he had applied and been accepted as a contestant in a quiz show. Because I was curious to learn more, I stopped by to see him. He lived in an upstairs room in a private home. The rent was nominal. As I climbed the stairs, I thought of how Tom was probably negotiating them with increasing difficulty and that he really should overcome his reluctance to consider a home for the aged. When I arrived at his door, Tom was eager to show me a letter of congratulations for having been accepted as a future contestant. As far as I could tell, it was a correspondence contest of sorts. The letter had been mailed from a Chicago address.

Tom let it be known throughout the congregation that he had been accepted in a quiz contest and that he had high hopes of making "a bundle," all of which he would give to the church. Passing the plate on Sundays was always a painful experience for him because he could put so little in it. Now he passed it with an inward smile, knowing that one day soon he might become the biggest giver of all.

Every day he studied the encyclopedia, the Bible, and whatever else he thought might help him become a winner. One day he received the expected letter. He was informed, by way of more congratulations, that he had been selected to move up to the next level as a contestant. Some others had been eliminated. To move up he would have to buy a dictionary, which would help him in his preparations and which was being offered to him at half price. Once more he called me to share the good news. Once more I climbed the stairs where he lived to see the letter for myself. I suspected that it was a scheme to separate people from their money. Tom refused to believe that, and bought a dictionary he could not really afford, not even at half price.

In due time he received another letter of congratulations, telling him that his name had been selected to move up to the final level of contestants—from where he could be launched into the actual contest. To rise to this highest level he would have to buy a book of biographies of famous people. He would be able to send for it at half price. Once more he called me. Once more I climbed the stairs. It was depressing to see Tom on the hook, abused and bilked. Yet once more he would not accept my warning. He bought the biographies, which were as cheaply bound as the dictionary he was studying.

It was then that I did something I should have done sooner. I knew just the right person in the congregation with whom to share my suspicions. That person made work of calling the Better Business Bureau of Chicago, or something similar, and that was that.

Tom agreed, soon after, to let the deacons help him with arrangements to move into a home for the aged. He was walking with increasing difficulty. He was 87. At first he didn't like the home. He said, "There's nothing but old people here." He was still young at heart and on the growing edge of life. But there he lived out his days, eating better than before and dreaming of what might have been. He had wanted so much to make "a bundle" and give it to the church. He never did. But I think the Lord accepted that bundle that never was with a "Well done, good and faithful servant."

Dick

He was 85 and poverty was his lot. He was small of stature. His white hair, in a crewcut, was matched by a bristly but well-trimmed beard. His manner was courtly. When he shook my hand at the church door after services, he always bowed slightly and clicked his heels. He bowed in similar fashion to others he greeted. The ladies considered him gallant, European-style. His clothes, although worn, were always clean and neat. He wore well-polished shoes, which he had obtained at the Salvation Army store. Unless you looked down, you might easily overlook the fact that he had cut the toe sections off because the shoes were a size too small.

He told me he was a stockbroker. He invited me to his office. He gave me his downtown address. We set a time: Monday evening at 8 p.m. He lived on the third floor in a block of downtown stores. I looked up at a window with letters in gold: "Dr. B. Physician." Sure that I had the wrong address, I went up anyway.

Dick was standing at the top of the stairs waiting to greet me. He was in his Sunday dress but wearing a green eyeshade. We walked through a reception room and into the office of "Dr. B. Physician." A chair awaited me. Dick sat in the swivel chair in front of an old-fashioned roll-top desk whose cubicles were all empty. On the desk stood a quart of milk and a box of cookies. Dick had purchased them for our refreshments. As usual, he bowed and clicked his heels. He was the soul of deference as he called me "Dominee."

But what in the world were we doing in Dr. B.'s inner sanctum? What was Dick doing seated at his desk? I felt like an intruder except for the fact of Dick's overwhelming hospitality. I needed some quick answers. I covered my confusion with a casual opener. I said, "Tell me about yourself." Since I was a new pastor, it was a logical request. Dick opened the box of cookies. He poured milk into two tubular-looking containers. On some shelves I saw what looked like old-fashioned jars, which probably contained the healing waters of a bygone day.

Dick began at the beginning. He said he had been born in "the old country"—The Netherlands—and that he was an illegitimate son of Queen Emma's prince consort (Queen Emma was the mother of Queen Wilhelmina, who was the mother of Queen Juliana, who was the mother of Queen Beatrix). When I expressed surprise, he said, "Let me show you some letters and papers." I was impressed. As I examined the evidence, I went from doubter to believer. "You see," he said with a smile, "I'm royalty—in a way." He poured me another tube of milk. I munched on cookies as he told me how his unwed mother was shunned, and of his sailing, in steerage, to America. As I listened, I began to understand why he conducted himself in such a courtly manner, and why he always clicked his well-polished open-toe shoes.

The story of his origin could easily have been the subject of conversation the whole evening, except for the fact that there was more mystery to uncover. At a moment I thought appropriate, and with most of the milk and cookies ingested, I asked him what in the world we were doing sitting in Dr. B.'s office. This became the introduction to another astonishing tale.

During the Depression Dick had no work. He got sick. A friend arranged an appointment with Dr. B., but Dick couldn't pay. He told me all of this in some detail. What followed was touching.

When he couldn't pay, Dr. B. made an arrangement with him. Dr. B. invited him to live in his reception room. In return he would keep the reception room and office clean. He could be a sort of night watchman. For these services he would have lodging and a modest stipend. But there were some stipulations, the chief of which was that he would have to be off the premises by 9:00 a.m. and not return until after 5:30 p.m. During these hours Dr. B. would be in his office seeing patients. Dick agreed; for years now he had been sleeping in the reception room—out by 9:00 and in after 5:30.

A pity the milk was all gone. "But," I stammered, "but, but what do you do all day from 9:00 in the morning to 5:30 in the afternoon?" He said that at first he had haunted the downtown library. Then he became interested in the stock market. He went daily to a nearby place where he could track the stock market and chart its progress or regress. He kept close track of all sorts of companies. He asked whether I wanted to see what had happened that day. He took out some graph papers he had in a notebook. I noticed how neatly everything was recorded in good old European penmanship. For writing he wore the green eyeshade.

He told me more. He said that over the years he had become an expert in stocks. He said that there was one wealthy person in our congregation who sought his advice frequently and who paid him a modest sum. "Do you advise others too?" I asked. "No," he said, "just the one man in our church. But what he gives me, in addition to what I get from Dr. B., is enough for me to get along on." He smiled. He said, "I can even buy some extras, like the milk and cookies for tonight."

After further talk, I said a prayer and left. It had been a remarkable evening. In bed, reflecting on it all, I marveled at his story and at the ways of God. And I thought, "What a fine man that Dr. B. must be!"

A year later, in my study in church, I was making a sermon and hoping that I would not be interrupted. But the secretary buzzed. There was an elderly gentleman to see me. Would it be all right? His name was Dr. B.

I had never met the man, although I had thought of him more than once. I went to greet him and ushered him to a chair opposite my desk. I wondered if something was wrong with Dick. Before Dr. B. could speak I told him that I knew what he was doing for our mutual friend and how generous it was. As I spoke, I noted the fact that he was well-preserved for a man of apparently advanced years.

"Dick is my reason for coming," he said. He continued. "Pastor, I am 92 years old. For twelve years now I have wanted to retire, but I can't. I haven't had a patient for years, but I still go to my office every weekday from nine to five. I go there to get away from my sister—that's the best way to get along with her. But mostly, I maintain my office for Dick. If I close it, where will he go?"

Dr. B. was unburdening himself to me even though he really didn't know me at all.

He continued, "I'd really like to go to Florida. I have never been to Florida. People half my age go to Florida. I've certainly got the money to go to there. But I feel that I have to maintain my office for Dick and keep an eye on him." He paused. I asked, "Is there anything I can do to help?" Dr. B. said that he was hoping that something could be done. He said that Dick was getting older, and that he should probably live somewhere where assistance was available to him. "But," he added, "I'm afraid Dick will have a heart attack if I tell him that I want to close shop. He considers it his mission in life to take care of my office and me."

I said that I agreed that something should be done and that I was willing to help. Dr. B. thanked me and left. He seemed a bit relieved. I called a deacon who had been close to Dick and told him about it. That evening I went to see Dick. I said, "I think you should consider letting the deacons help you find another situation. You are getting older. I think you deserve to go somewhere where the living is easier. There's a fine home for the aged in town. You would like it there." I didn't tell him about Dr. B.'s call on me and what his wishes were.

I braced myself for Dick's reply. I could hardly believe my ears. He said, "I'd love to go, but I can't. Dr. B. needs me. What would he do without me? He's getting older, you know. But, oh, how tired I am of sleeping on that hard couch in the reception room." He was astonished when I told him that Dr. B. had spoken to me about closing his office.

And so it was all straightened out. Imagine! Here were two old men who had been sacrificing, albeit reluctantly, for each other. Each one thought only of the need of the other. So Dick was moved to a home for the elderly. Dr. B. closed his office and went to Florida. The first time I called on Dick in his new surroundings, he made me feel the bed. "Much better than that old couch," he said. On a table I saw some neglected stock market charts. On the dresser there was a postcard from Florida. On it Dr. B. had written, "Having a wonderful time." Dick was having a wonderful time as well.

For years thereafter, walking downtown to the weekly Rotary meeting, I would look up to a third-floor window in a block of stores, to see some fading letters in gold.

"Dr. B. Physician." But the doctor wasn't in anymore.

Neither was the night watchman.

Harry

Harry should have been given a medal for being in church every Sunday. He was old and plagued with arthritis. It would have been much easier for him to stay at home and listen to a sermon on the radio.

It had been suggested that we put our services on the air, but the committee that had researched the idea recommended against it. It was a time when many services were broadcast by radio. On Sundays, each turn of the dial brought another sermon. A few shut-ins in our congregation listened to seven or eight sermons every Sunday. I admired them. At the same time, I wondered sometimes whether listening to so many messages could cause a kind of spiritual indigestion.

But Harry denied himself worshiping by radio. As long as it was humanly possible, he would be in church, even though dressing, driving, and walking from the parking lot to his accustomed seat in church was a daunting and painful exercise.

Even as a young man, Harry had been devout. He grew up in his native land, The Netherlands, and had married a Christian girl. Together they prayed about moving to America, but the Lord, it seemed, did not open the way. Even so, Harry kept himself poised for the journey, should the Lord present even the smallest of possibilities. When it was suggested to him that he travel to America alone, make some money, and then send for his wife, he went. Both favored the plan. He said goodbye to his wife, who was pregnant. Soon he would have saved enough money to pay passage for her and the baby.

Alas, the year was 1929. The stock market failed, and America plummeted into the deepest economic depression in its history. Harry could find no work. He stood in the soup lines. A letter from Holland informed him that his wife had died in childbirth. The baby—his baby—a girl, had been taken home by his wife's sister.

Time passed. Harry found sporadic work at meager wages. His situation improved a little. He married again. It would be better to have a wife when he sent for his daughter. His second wife also died, and Harry became increasingly disabled by arthritis.

Friends helped. Harry was given some light tasks of a janitorial nature in the church. With his big mane of beautiful white hair he presented an imposing presence. As I looked out at the congregation, it was hard to miss him.

When I came to the church as the new pastor, I began making get-acquainted calls, first on the shut-ins, and then on the elderly in their homes. It wasn't long before I called on Harry. We hit it off well. He said that he loved my sermons. He had never lost his Dutch accent. The word "love" sounded like "lawf." He lawfd my sermons. And every Sunday, after the morning worship hour, he would shake my hand, pause, and say, "Now dat was en sermon!"

I must honestly say that his flattery didn't turn my head. I knew that each and every message I delivered did not deserve the accolades and encomiums he heaped upon them. Not even the best preachers, my superiors in the pulpit, can hit a home run every time they preach. It is true that sometimes I did hit one, so to speak, out of the park. But sometimes I struck out, and sometimes I was grateful to get away with a scratch single. But even on the days I struck out, Harry would pause at the door, shake my hand, and say, "Now dat was en sermon!" And then he would generally declare his love for me. "I lawf you."

Harry could not have managed in his little house had it not been for a neighbor lady who was an angel in disguise. She looked in on him every day, did his shopping, his laundry, and a little light housekeeping. Her first task every morning was to hop over to Harry's for a moment to help him with his socks and shoes. He was able to dress and carry on his ablutions by himself. But socks and shoes were something else. One day, his angel of a neighbor called me. She was going out of town for a week. Could I pop in every morning on my way to church to help Harry with his socks and shoes?

The seminary I had attended had a very limited curriculum. It had never offered a course on how to help people with their socks and shoes. If it had offered such a course, and if I had taken it, I am sure I would have been given a failing mark. That is because I am all thumbs when it comes to helping people physically. Nor do I have the disposition for it.

I told the angel of mercy that I would do my best. For a whole week, I helped Harry with his socks and shoes. The first day I looked at his toes and decided they were ugly. That night I looked at my own. They were ugly too. I think all toes, although necessary appendages for walking, are ugly. As I knelt before Harry, mornings and evenings, putting on or removing his socks and shoes, he would sometimes pat me on the head. I hated that. Then he would say, "I lawf you." My response was that he needed to get the ball rolling and get himself into a home for the aged. The deacons would help. But Harry liked it where he was.

Meanwhile, in the Netherlands, Harry had an adult daughter he had never seen. They corresponded regularly. He told me that she was married and had two sons—grandsons he had also never seen. Their pictures were prominently displayed on a table. His son-in-law, I learned, was a mechanic. He worked for the government, maintaining government cars. One day, when I was helping Harry with his socks and shoes, he told me that it was his daughter's birthday. She was forty.

I told someone in the congregation that Harry's daughter, a daughter he had never seen, had just turned forty, The remark planted a seed. The seed grew. A dozen or so families pitched in to contribute enough money to fly Harry to Holland to meet his daughter. The daughter was contacted. She was ecstatic. Harry was hesitant until we told him that the airline people would take care of him all the way. Arrangements were made for a two-month stay. His sponsors and I went to the airport to see him off. I said a prayer. Harry was gone. His angel neighbor was happy to get away for a while without having to worry about him.

A month later my telephone rang. It was Harry. Had something gone wrong? He wasn't due back for another month. He asked if I could come over. I went. Harry told me that his daughter had met him at the airport, and that it was lawf at first sight. In the following week they had so much to tell each other. His daughter, a very caring person, thought that it was wrong that an ocean should separate them. She wanted to take care of him. Harry needed no persuading. Now that, at long last, father and daughter were together, Harry wanted to keep it that way. They were agreed.

The matter was quickly resolved. Too quickly, in my estimation. Harry took the first plane back. He wanted to liquidate his few possessions and terminate all connections, in order to fly back as soon as possible to take up residence with his beloved daughter and her family. At long last he had family.

I urged Harry to change his mind. I said that in my opinion it was a wrong decision. He was too old to be transplanted. I said you can't teach an old dog new tricks. He was set in his ways, and his daughter and family would find it hard to adjust to a permanent boarder. He had a name and a place where he was. The deacons could move him into a home for the aged where he would be cared for and where his friends could visit him. I said that he was on a honeymoon with his daughter, but honeymoons don't last. I mustered all the arguments I could think of to convince Harry to stay, but he would not be dissuaded. He was a stubborn old coot. He said

I didn't understand. He said that it was the Lord's will that father and daughter be reunited.

Harry sold his car for a pittance. A few other belongings brought a little money. The angel neighbor arranged for a garage sale. Most of what was left went to the Salvation Army. Once again, we brought him to the airport. Once again, I offered a parting prayer. We embraced. We said our next meeting would be in heaven.

At first I missed his presence. No longer, when preaching, would I see that beautiful mane of white hair on a man who listened intently, who thought all my sermons were home runs, and who lawfd me. But I was wrong to think that I had ended my pastoral dealings with him.

It was almost a year later that I received a letter from Holland. It was from Harry's daughter, and it contained a tale of woe. She wrote that things had not been going well in the family since her father had moved in. At first everything was wonderful. But the situation had gone from wonderful to tolerable and from tolerable to impossible. Her sons resented the fact that their room was now Grandpa's room and that they had to settle for lesser accommodations. Their house, she wrote, was really too small for the five of them.

Furthermore, she continued, her father was not easy to live with. Everything seemed to have to revolve around him. She gave an example. It was always their custom to have friends over for coffee after the Sunday morning church services. They were still doing this, but her father always dominated the conversation. And he was forever telling people how much better things were in Grand Rapids, Michigan.

Harry's daughter wrote that her husband could hardly stand it anymore. On the previous Sunday, matters had come to a head. Her father had again said to their visitors how much better everything was in Grand Rapids, Michigan. It was the last straw for the husband. He exploded, right in front of their guests. He said, "Well, if everything is so much better in Grand Rapids, Michigan, why don't you just get up and go back there?" "Reverend," wrote the daughter, "it was most embarrassing. Our guests didn't know what to say or where to look. They left as quickly as they could. My husband and my father refused to speak to each other the rest of the day."

I tried to imagine the scene. I was accustomed to seeing Harry in an altogether different setting. It was hard for me to cast a man who was so full of lawf in the role of a culprit. I picture him with his beautiful mane of white hair. I resumed my reading of the letter.

The daughter explained that her father was seeking to persuade them all to move to Grand Rapids, Michigan. The boys would have a better future in the land of opportunity. His son-in-law, being a good automobile mechanic, would surely make a living in the land of automobiles. She was asking for my advice. Did I see their moving to Grand Rapids, Michigan as a possibility? Was it a good idea? In any case, they would not consider relocating unless there was a prior assurance that her husband would be gainfully employed.

She asked for my honest opinion. She apologized for burdening me with her request. Surely I had enough to do, she wrote, and more important matters with which to contend. At the same time, she didn't know where else to turn for light, except to the Lord, and she was doing that already.

There was more. She requested that, should I reply, I send my answer to the address of a close friend who lived several houses up the street. She said that she was embarrassed to tell me the reason. She explained that during the day, when she and her husband were both working and the boys were at school, that her father sat by the window, watching pedestrians and cars, and looking for the postman for possible letters from Grand Rapids, Michigan. That wasn't so bad, except that when the mail arrived, he opened not only his, but theirs. Repeated requests for him to mind his own business and to respect their privacy fell on deaf ears. He continued to open their mail, read their letters, and examine their bills. It was an intolerable habit, but she could do nothing about it.

I decided to sleep on her letter before sending a reply. I went to a member of the congregation who had a Ford agency, and was given the promise of a job in the event that Harry would move back to Grand Rapids, Michigan, with his family in tow. I sought the advice of some friends whose opinion I respected. Theirs coincided with my own growing conviction that Harry's family should stay put.

I wrote my letter, taking care to phrase my thoughts correctly. I told Harry's daughter that if they decided to move to Grand Rapids, Michigan, that the congregation would do all it could to help. My parishioners had outdone themselves a number of times, with people coming from Cuba and Hungary, in finding and furnishing apartments. I was sure that they would do as much and more for Harry and his family. I also gave assurance that her husband would have a job as a mechanic in a Ford agency. I offered to do what I could to help with whatever legal matters might arise.

But I also added that, in my opinion, they ought to remain where they were. Her boys were of an age when uprooting them might not serve them well. Her husband, upon retirement, would receive a good pension. As far as her father was concerned, I wrote that she might consider moving him to a home for the aged. I added that I had visited some old aunts and uncles in her country and that I had been impressed with the excellence of the old people's homes where they lived. I wrote that they were better, on the whole, than what we had in America.

I sealed the letter and mailed it in care of her friend who lived up the street, according to her request. I felt that I had given the whole matter my best shot. I was also very glad that my advice, which was contrary to Harry's wishes, would not fall into his hands.

About three weeks later, the shortest man in my congregation, who also had the loudest voice, came to my study. He was in his seventies, and retired. Tom and Dick and the other members of The Brotherhood could never outshout him in the theological free-for-alls that frequently took place on the first and third Mondays of every month. His name was Bonjenoor. He had been a self-styled foot doctor. He had printed business cards which, despite his retirement, he was still distributing to all and sundry. They rhymed. They said:

Foot-sore?

See Bonjenoor!

Bonjenoor had been one of Harry's close friends. He was one of the several who had contributed to Harry's trip to see his daughter. Since Harry had moved to the old country, he and Bonjenoor had maintained a brisk interchange of letters. Now the shortest man in my church with the loudest voice was in my study, placing a letter on my desk and inviting me to read it. It was a letter to him from Harry.

"Read it," he said, and added, "You won't like it." I read:

"Dear Bonjenoor:

"Eppinga is a snake in the grass. Eppinga should be exposed for what he is. Eppinga should be deposed from the ministry of the church. Eppinga is a stabber in the back. Eppinga. . . . "

I read on. The whole long paragraph was filled with invective. I had never known that Harry could be so eloquent. But was this the man who "lawfd" me, whose shoes I had been worthy to tie, and who considered every sermon I preached to be a home run? I read on. I came to the last sentence in the paragraph: "Eppinga is a Jezebel."

"Now hold on, Harry," I thought. I certainly didn't think I was all those things Harry said I was, but I was most emphatically no Jezebel—the worst woman in the Old Testament. I was a man! Not a woman!

With sadness I handed back the letter to the shortest man in my church with the loudest voice. "Something must have gone wrong," I said.

I didn't have to wait long to learn what it was. The next day a letter arrived from Harry's daughter. It was full of apologies. She explained what had happened. When my letter to her came into the hands of her postman, he assumed the writer had gotten the address wrong. So he elected to bring the letter directly to her house instead of delivering it to the friend up the street. Her father, who was waiting for the mail, wondered what in the world was going on. He opened and read the letter. He learned that his daughter had written secretly to me and that I was answering contrary to his wishes and making an end run around him by addressing the letter to a friend up the street. When the daughter came home, there had been a terrible scene. Harry was now accusing her of stabbing him in the back. What kind of treatment was that for an old man full of arthritis! "If only," she wrote, "the postman had left the letter with my friend up the street."

I did not write Harry a letter. But I did send his daughter a note. I sent it to her address, knowing that Harry would open it. I wrote it in such a way that it might pour oil on the troubled waters. I said that Harry had his virtues. I hoped she would see them. I assured her again that, if they still decided to come, they could expect to find everything better in Grand Rapids, Michigan.

About a year later I had been chosen, along with a few other clergymen, to represent our denomination at the Synod of a sister church's assembly in The Netherlands. At the end of the first week I was invited to be the guest of a professor in the very town where Harry, his daughter, and her family lived. Since my note to his daughter, I had had no further contact. Nor had the shortest man in my church with the loudest voice kept me abreast of things.

While I was at Sunday dinner in the house of the professor, someone came to the door asking to see me. Excusing myself from the table, and meeting my caller, I was astonished. The lady introduced herself. She was Harry's daughter. She said she had heard that I was in town. She apologized for the interruption and said she would be brief. She said she could not resist the attempt to meet me in person and to thank me again for all I had done. "Your advice was good," she said, and added, "It would have been a mistake for us to move to Grand Rapids, Michigan."

"And your father?" I asked. She said that her father was well and living nearby in a home for the aged. She hesitated, then asked, "Would you have time to call on my father?"

Call on Harry when he thought I was "a snake in the grass," and, worst of all, "a Jezebel"? I thanked her for calling on me. As for my calling on her father, that was a different matter. I said, "I probably will not have the time." I hedged, because I didn't want to make a promise I might not keep.

The meetings that I was delegated to attend didn't resume until the following Tuesday. That gave me Monday to nose around town. My inclination was not to call on Harry. But, as I wandered aimlessly about, providence led me past a fine-looking building with a sign that said that it was a home for the aged. A beautiful place. Was that where Harry lived? I walked in. To the right of the entrance hall there was a very attractive lounge. On the far side of it, I saw a beautiful white mane of hair. It was, indeed, Harry. Another gentleman sat opposite him at a small table. They were playing chess. With some hesitation I approached. Harry was looking down, deep in thought, contemplating his next move. I edged closer. He saw my feet. He looked up.

"Reverend Eppinga," he exclaimed. He clapped his hands. He smiled from ear to ear. He reached out for my hand. He said, "Reverend Eppinga, I lawf you!"

It was a wonderful reunion. I was introduced to his playing partner. Someone brought us coffee. I looked around. The lounge was well-appointed: windows, curtains, bookshelves with all manner of reading material—what a home! I said, "Harry, this is a wonderful place."

"Yes," he replied. Then he said, "But not as good as in Grand Rapids, Michigan."

Hospitality

There was a lady in the Old Testament whose door was always open to Reverend Elisha. As Peter advised his readers years later, she was much given to hospitality (1 Pet. 4:9). Indeed, she had a special room built and furnished for the prophet to use whenever he was in the neighborhood (2 Kings 4:10). I consider her, together with her New Testament counterpart, Martha (Luke 10:40), to be the patron saints of all those who harbor strangers. And clergy.

The first church I served as a student pastor was in Philadelphia, Pennsylvania. I soon discovered that the ladies of that church were determined to put meat on my skinny frame. One of them, a corseted spinster who played the piano for the services, had just acquired the newly invented Waring blender. I think she bought it with me in mind. It was the first thing she hauled out of the cupboard when I called. Using it, she reduced spinach, carrots, and other vegetables into a greenish milky mix. I had to force it down while she watched every swallow. It would have been bad manners to refuse. Such hospitality! One must sacrifice, I thought, for ministry.

When I came to my last charge, my predecessor warned me, "When you go calling, accept only a glass of water." I forgot to heed his advice. I found myself in trouble on the very first call I made. I ran into a chocolate cake baked just for me. It was a harbinger of things to come. For many years I climbed mountains of cake and swam through oceans of coffee. Still, like Pharaoh's lean cows eating the fat ones while still remaining lean (Gen. 41:17-21), I stayed skinny.

Peter Cartwright, the backwoods preacher of the last century, could not have survived his circuit riding days without the Marthas of his time. Nor could many an itinerant evangelist since. And what stories some of them had to tell! I have never really believed the tale of the guest preacher who visited a family whose practice it was to eat out of a large common bowl in the center of the table. This preacher spooned up a small bone with his food. He shifted it from cheek to cheek, not knowing what to do with it. Noticing this, his host told him to put it back in the pot. He said he'd already had it in his mouth twice. That story has *got* to be apocryphal. But the one about the flies is not. An older minister, now gone to glory, told me about it. It was a hot summer day. There were no screens on the open windows. Fly paper, suspended from the ceiling, caught only the smallest fraction of the insects buzzing in the room. The bowl of rice on the table was black with them. My friend delved into the bowl from the side with his spoon upside down, mining the rice from the bottom of the bowl and shoveling it on to his plate, his spoon an upside down scoop.

He had more stories to tell. He could have written a book. One Saturday night he was the guest of a very poor couple. They lived in a two-room shack. He was scheduled to preach in their church the following morning. He took note of the one bedroom with the one bed. He wondered about the sleeping arrangements for the night, but he said nothing about it. Upon retiring he was told to sleep on the far side of the bed, leaving room for the host. The lady of the house stayed up. An hour or so later, she stole silently into the bedroom and got in on the near side of the bed, her husband in the middle. Three in a bed! Sunday morning she was the first to rise, stealing silently out of the room. The minister, inwardly upset, pretended, but didn't sleep a wink all night. At breakfast no one said anything about it. After the service—and dinner—the minister declined the hospitable invitation to remain for another night.

One of my seminary professors shared his experiences with us one evening in a humorous speech entitled "Beds I Have Slept in—or *on.*" It was the early 1920s. He was a seminary student. He had a preaching assignment. The church was twelve miles outside of town. Because this distance was longer than what was deemed a Sabbath day's journey, he had to arrive on Saturday and leave on Monday. For this reason no seminary classes were held on Mondays. The professors or students who had preached out of town needed to uphold the fourth commandment by traveling on Saturday and Monday. Never on Sunday!

It was the dead of winter. Our professor, then a student, arrived at the home of his host and hostess on Saturday afternoon. The temperature was below zero. At bedtime he was ushered upstairs to the guest room. Wonderful! But the bed was too short, the blankets too few, and there was no heat in the room. He spent a miserable night, sleepless and cold. When it was time to preach in the morning service, he was not half thawed out. He was, however, well warmed for the afternoon service. That evening he retired again to the bed that was too short, the blankets that were too few, and the room that was too cold. The next morning, seated in the interurban train that took him back to town, his frozen brain vowed never to repeat his experience. If possible.

The following year his preaching assignment took him back to the same church. He hoped against hope that he would be lodged with another family. Alas, the couple who had housed him the previous year asked to have him again. They had enjoyed hosting him and looked forward to his return.

Once more it was the dead of winter. It was even colder than the year before. It was the same guest room. The bed was still too short. The blankets were still too few. And the room, unlike the rest of the house, was still unheated. Once again he suffered, sleepless and cold. But in the course of that wretched night he made a bold decision. He would not sleep in that bed another night.

While preaching in the morning service he was, again, only half thawed out. He was, again, well warmed for the afternoon service, after which he announced to his astonished hosts that he was going home. "But it is Sunday," they said. "And anyway, the interurban train doesn't run on Sundays!" But their guest was not to be deterred. He thanked them kindly for their hospitality. Then, to their consternation, he said goodbye and trudged home twelve long miles through snow and ice. It was hard. But it was better than sleeping in a bed that was too short, with blankets that were too few, and in a room whose temperature was colder than the temperature out of doors.

The following Tuesday two elders from the church twelve miles out of town called on the seminary president. They were there to lodge a protest against the student preacher of the previous Sunday. He had broken the fourth commandment. He had traveled more than a Sabbath day's journey. What sort of example was that? The infraction of the rule was soberly noted. A two-week suspension from classes was imposed as punishment by the faculty.

Today the punishment sounds harsh. Extremely Sabbatarian! Still, compared to today, when many worshipers leave church for Sunday brunches and buffets, beaches and golf courses, there is something to be said for the Sabbaths of a previous generation.

I recall a situation in which I was also warmly, yet coldly, received. It was in the far North. A long train ride had brought me to my destination on Saturday evening. I was heartily received at the station. I was told that I would have the honor of being the first minister to sleep in the new parsonage.

This offer sounded better than it turned out to be. The parsonage was not completely finished. The janitor and his wife were living in the large kitchen. It was warm and cozy there. We drank tea together and ate some delicious raisin buns. Then I was ushered to the master bedroom. It was below zero outside and even colder than that inside. The bed was not too short, and there seemed to be enough blankets. But I wondered how I would fare. I wrote my name in the heavy frost on the windows. I tried to rehearse my sermon, but the cold discouraged all preparation. I ended up sleeping fully dressed under a pile of blankets. There was a chamber pot under the bed. In the morning the janitor brought me some hot water for the old-fashioned wash bowl in the corner on a stand. I stood on my frozen tube of toothpaste but could get nothing out.

The church was next door. My experience there proved to be much different than the bone-chilling night spent in the parsonage. The pulpit was positioned unusually high, near the ceiling. There were ladder-like steps leading up to it. Inside the main door of the church stood a wood stove. During the service the janitor kept feeding the flames to keep the parishioners alive. Even so, they were freezing to death despite their overcoats and beaver hats. All warm air from the stove rose over their heads to the ceiling. That's where I was. My head got so hot I was almost wishing for my cold bedroom. That night the thoughts of that hot pulpit helped to keep me alive as, once more, I crawled under a pile of blankets fully clothed, with my tube of toothpaste in one of my armpits. After all, one must do what is necessary to survive. Like my professor, I had been warmly, but also coldly, received.

I remember when, as a visiting preacher, I was brought to a motel instead of to someone's house. Surprise! I enjoyed the accommodations. The privacy was wonderful, but I missed the fellowship. Still, it is possible to be lodged with a family and have no fellowship at all. I remember staying with an older couple in whose church I was preaching every night for a week-long evangelistic campaign. They were simple, monosyllabic folk, and reluctant conversationalists. They were obviously ill-at-ease in my presence, even though I tried to make them comfortable with small talk. I almost had the feeling that I was the host and not the guest. They seemed tense and intimidated by my presence. On several occasions I retired early to ease the situation, though I was reluctant to do so. My bedroom was cheerless. No pictures on the wall. Just a solitary bare lightbulb hanging from the center of the ceiling.

One evening, trying to manufacture some conversation, I made a reference to a picture hanging above the mantel. I lied. I said it was a lovely thing. I couldn't very well say that I thought it was ugly. It was just an attempt to break the unendurable silence and get some conversation going. To no avail. They said, "Thank you," and that was that.

I was glad to leave at the end of the week. We said our goodbyes. They gave me a package. I opened it on the plane ride home. It contained a note. It said that they were simple folk and that it had been an honor to have such an educated man as myself as their guest. They asked me to accept their present. It was the ugly picture that had hung over the mantel and which they said "I had so much admired." I was touched. I also thought that my sin had found me out.

In my first charge I was sometimes called on to supply the pulpit of a small and struggling congregation nearby. It met in the local YWCA. Its members consisted of a few individuals, a widow with small children, an elderly couple, a few more small families, and one very large one with countless children. These Sundays were always pleasant experiences for me. I was always invited to dinner between the morning and the afternoon services by the husband and wife who had the countless and unfailingly well-behaved children. They were people of very modest means. They lived close to a railroad track where passing steam engines shook the dishes off the table—to the delight of the host, who was a train buff. He was a man who was endlessly awed by the power of the locomotives that shivered the timbers of his house. He was also a very devout man and a leader of the small congregation of which he and his family were members.

I always looked forward to the dinners at the large dining room table which we all crowded around. The food was always wonderful and plentiful and the conversations unfailingly interesting. I was made to feel as if I were a part of the family. The afternoon service began at 2:30 p.m. I could have stayed at their table well past that time.

One Sunday we were all having such great fun around the dinner table that we forgot about the time. Suddenly, my host, shocked, announced that it was 2:20 p.m. We had a bare ten minutes to vacate the house and race to the YWCA to get to the church on time. We jumped, fell over each other, abandoned all the dishes on the table, and rushed to our cars. A few of the children piled into my car. Arriving in record time, we ran breathlessly into the meeting room of the YWCA—they to their chairs and me to the pulpit. It was 2:30

p.m. on the dot. We had made it! The funny thing was that we were the only ones there. The few individuals, the widow with her little ones, the elderly couple, and the few more families never showed. It was just me and my host family.

We could have saved ourselves a lot of rushing around. We could have held that afternoon service around the dining room table.

In the earlier years of my ministry I corresponded regularly with many of my seminary classmates. Some of them had gone off to serve churches in Iowa. They wrote sometimes about cows and the smell of pigs. Our parish was entirely devoid of such creatures because we were surrounded by industry. And having been city people all our lives, my wife and I didn't long for the Iowa farmlands. But we had second thoughts when our friends wrote and told us that their parishioners were supplying them with meat. When one of my former classmates wrote that someone had brought him half a cow, I couldn't resist exclaiming "Holy cow!" to my wife.

The fact was that on our small salary we couldn't afford meat very often. We ate it once or twice a week. We tried horse meat once, because it was cheap, but we didn't like it. I tried fishing, but never caught anything. It was difficult to avoid the sin of envy as I conjured up pictures of former classmates rolling in pork chops. One day, however, the score was evened a little. A couple from our church came calling. The man was carrying a chicken. It was alive!

"For you," he said. How wonderful! Meat! I didn't know how to take his offering. By the feet? My wife invited them in for tea. I brought the squawking chicken to the basement and, not knowing what else to do, deposited it in the coal bin. Then I went upstairs and joined the tea party.

The man worked for the Ford Motor Company. He proceeded to tell me all about it. He said that Fords were much better than Chevrolets. I asked what was so bad about Chevrolets, and he answered, "Well, for one thing, they look like flying birds coming at you because they have floppy fenders." I had never seen any Chevrolets with floppy fenders, but, grateful for his gift, I decided to grant him his point. His wife was of the same mind. He expanded his criticisms of Chevrolets to include all General Motors products. My wife, having about as little knowledge of the automobile world as I had, but also grateful for the chicken, joined me in agreeing to the shortcomings of General Motors. Our visitors both took a refill of their tea cups. Meanwhile, I was fast losing interest in the subject of automobiledom.

There were two concerns that distracted my attention, and those concerns mounted with each passing moment. The first was that I would soon have to leave to conduct a midweek service at a church fifty miles away. I would have to get there in an old General Motors product which, if it didn't have floppy fenders, had floppy everything else. My second concern was the chicken in our coal bin. How would I kill it? How would I even catch it? I was simply no good at that sort of thing. In fact, I had never killed a chicken in my life.

A few weeks earlier, another member of our church had taken me hunting. He furnished a gun and bought me a license. I had an immediate crisis as soon as we began to track through a wooded area. I had a rabbit in my sights but I couldn't pull the trigger. Was he a daddy rabbit? Was mommy rabbit at home with the kids? How could I possibly break up that little family? My friend told me to shoot, but I froze and never went hunting again. But here I was, sipping tea and listening to a seminar on the deficiencies of General Motors and the superiority of the Ford Motor Company. And all the while a chicken, on death row, in our coal bin!

I decided to make a clean breast of it. I explained that I had to leave soon for a service that evening fifty miles away, and that I had never killed a chicken, and could he do it for me—right now?

It was the funniest thing our guests had ever heard. They laughed loudly, stopped to look at each other, and laughed again! "He never killed a chicken," the man told his wife. "He never killed a chicken?" she asked her husband. I laughed right along with them, although I didn't feel like it. "Sure," he said, finally. With the superiority of a Ford man—I shall omit the details of the execution—he killed the chicken. They left soon after that. High time too! I had fifty miles ahead of me.

I returned around midnight. Entering the back door, I met my wife coming up from the basement. She looked worn out. Drained. Alarmed, I asked whether there was something wrong. The furnace, perhaps? It had been giving us trouble. "No," she said, and then told me that she had spent the whole long evening plucking the chicken. Pulling out one feather at a time. And she had to clean out its insides too. Yuck!

Not long after, our expert on the inadequacies of Chevrolets was at our door again with his wife and another chicken. This time the chicken was dead. We drank more tea together. We were the souls of hospitality. After all, there was a meat shortage at our house. We were able to divert our guests' attention away from the sins of General Motors long enough to learn how to clean and pluck a chicken. I wrote to my friend in Iowa who was rolling in pork chops and who kept boasting about eating high on the hog. I said that we were not doing too badly ourselves. We were dining on fowl. Out of the goodness of my heart I also shared some recently acquired knowledge of the respective merits and demerits of certain makes of cars.

Meanwhile we were having lots of other visitors, especially during the summer months. Living near the main Ford plant and Henry Ford's Greenfield Village, a national attraction, we received numbers of visitors from other states. Among them were members of our small denomination. They would look us up. These people were total strangers. But those were the days when the members of our Christian Reformed denomination felt closely knit together, no matter how many the separating miles, and no matter how scattered they were throughout the country. Driving hundreds of miles to see Greenfield Village, it simply wouldn't do to leave without stopping in to greet the Christian Reformed minister who lived in the area. They rang our doorbell, denominational Yearbook in hand. Consequently, we always had the teapot ready and cookies on hand (homemade or storebought, but, either way, not always easy on the budget).

One day the people with the chickens stopped by again. Alas, they were empty-handed. Still, I sensed an ill-concealed excitement. During tea and cookies, they came to the point. They had a cottage several hundred miles up North. They looked at each other with agreement in their faces. Then they looked at us and said that we could vacation in their cottage for a week at no cost to us. Quickly getting over our disappointment of no chicken, we poured some more tea. How wonderful! Thank you. Thank you!

Before their visit, we had decided to forego any kind of vacation because of a lack of funds. We had made the same decision the year before and for the same reason. Instead, I had painted a house during vacation time to augment our small income. My letter of call had said, "Convinced that the laborer is worthy of his hire, and in order to free you from all worldly care and avocation, we agree to pay you the annual sum of ____ dollars, in monthly installments." But, in spite of the members' sacrificial giving, we were scarcely freed from all worldly care and avocation. I had already looked around for another house to paint during our vacation time. But a free cottage up North for a whole week? Who could turn that down? We were profuse in our thanks. Leaving, and getting into their Ford, the man cast a scornful glance at our General Motors product and said, "I hope you make it." I wrote to my classmate in Iowa who was full of pork. We had something better. A vacation up North.

Our children soon tired of the trip. We still had miles to go, but they kept hopefully asking, "Are we there already?" Near the end of the wearying journey, we passed a small country church surrounded by parked cars. "What do you know?" exclaimed my wife. "A Christian Reformed church!" I didn't much care what it was, being more than anxious to arrive at our destination. In another fifteen minutes we were there.

The cottage had seen better days. It wasn't exactly lakefront property, but it was close enough. We hoped there would be time to give the children a ride in the rowboat before darkness set in. I put the key in the door, feeling like a king. I flung it open, turned to my wife and said "Entrée!" We all went inside. Alas, there was clutter everywhere. The kitchen sink was piled high with dirty dishes. Son number one emerged from the bathroom to tell me that the toilet had tipped over. "Honest," he said, "I didn't do it." My wife came out of the bedroom. She said there was a terrible odor there. She was sure a skunk had let go under the house or between the walls and then had died right there.

There was no ride in the rowboat that night to see the setting sun. Instead, there was a mountain of dishes to wash, a toilet to fix, and a bedroom to air out as best we could, not to mention a car to unload. We put the children to bed in a small room just large enough for a few bunks. We worked and worked, finally tumbling into bed well past the midnight hour. My wife hung her head over the side of the mattress, an open bottle of Airwick air freshener on the floor under her nose. A low-hanging branch of a tree kept scratching the roof in the wind. The sky finally began to lighten in the east. We fell asleep.

Finally!

At 7:30 a.m. the children were impatiently standing beside our bed. They wanted to go fishing. At 8:00 a.m. we heard someone pounding on the door. What day was it? Where were we? What was my wife doing with her head on the floor? A slightly disoriented preacher, standing in shorts, answered the knocking, two little boys peeking from behind him. The two men at the door were from the church we had passed, surrounded by the cars, the night before. I invited them in. After all, Peter had said, ". . . given to hospitality."

The men handed me an envelope. "Last night," one of them said, "we had a congregational meeting. We voted to call you as our minister." I felt that I should receive such an invitation dressed more properly, and excused myself to find my pants. I came back wearing swim trunks. I opened the letter and read it while wondering what had happened to my pants. It was the usual form letter. "Convinced that the laborer is worthy of his hire, and to free you from all worldly care and avocation . . . " "We heard you were coming," they said. "The owner of this cottage is a friend of ours. He called to say you would be here. What a coincidence! We had you on a list of three ministers to choose from, and last night you were chosen. Is your Missus here?"

I had reveled in the thought of getting away from church business and church talk and church work for a whole week. But here I was, listening to a description of their congregation's needs and to their hope that I would give their call my prayerful consideration.

I said I would be happy to offer them some coffee, but I didn't know if we had any or, if we did, how to make it in a strange kitchen. "Anyway," I said, "my Missus is still sleeping because we had a long trip and a late night." They understood. They offered prayer for me and the Missus and the children. When they left, they said they would be back to discuss matters further, and could I preach for them on the following Sunday? I smiled inwardly. That would be impossible because I had not taken a suit with me, or shirt or tie. Outwardly I thanked them for the invitation, taking care to be very clear about not being able to preach for them. I wanted desperately to have the following Sunday off. "And anyway," I said, "I have no sermons with me."

They left. My Missus appeared. She looked groggy. Too much Airwick in the lungs. I found my pants. I asked if she had taken any cookies along. I said, "I think we're going to need them." I told her what had transpired already so early in the morning. As it turned out, we needed lots of cookies. We spent our "mad money"—meant for splurging on a night out at a restaurant—on cookies. We needed them to entertain all the delegations that appeared at our door.

It began the first evening. I was going fishing. But the two men of the morning appeared with all the other members of the church council in tow. The following afternoon, the ladies representing the Ladies Aid came calling. Representatives of the Men's Society, the Young Peoples' Society, the Mission Society, plus individuals and couples, self-appointed; these and more kept coming throughout the week. All wonderful people. They drank coffee, tea, and Kool-aid. And they ate cookies.

Each day we practiced hospitality, squeezing a little fishing and swimming in here and there. On Saturday, a man about my size brought me his jacket, shirt, and tie. On Sunday I preached morning and evening and taught a Sunday school class. At noon we were the guests of some very hospitable people. We ate chicken! On Monday we went home. My Missus made sure we left the cottage spic and span. She also left a few Airwick air fresheners, strategically placed, here and there.

We came home. There was some mail. Bills. And a letter from Porky in Iowa. After careful consideration I declined the call to the church up North. Since then, I have often thought that it would have been a wonderful place for our children to grow up. Soon enough a Ford pulled up in front of the parsonage. It was the man with the Ph.D. in automobile knowledge. He and his wife were dropping in again. We drank tea and served cookies left over from up North. We thanked them for the free use of the cottage. We said we had kept busy every day. Never a dull moment! They looked pleased. They were good people—the very souls of hospitality.

This Is a Church—This Is a Steeple

JV was adamant. Our church building was not going to be leveled! It just needed fixing up. The beautiful sanctuary was irreplaceable! Generations had gathered in it for worship. They had been baptized in it, married in it, and buried from it. The place was hallowed! God's Word had been faithfully proclaimed from its pulpit. Its walls were sacred. If you listened carefully, they could tell you of songs sung and sermons preached.

JV was someone to be reckoned with. He was Mr. Congregation. He was kindly, but he could also be kindly despotic. If he said that the old building would not be replaced, it would, in all probability, not be replaced.

I was anxious to keep the peace in the congregation. Some of the members were growing restless. Not only was the old sanctuary tired and worn, it was also too small. A hundred people regularly sat in the lounge. There were children for whom the preacher was a loudspeaker box up on a wall. The congregation was becoming increasingly polarized. One group, led by JV, wanted the sanctuary repaired, whatever the expense. Those who objected said that the prohibitive cost of shoring up the sagging south wall would still, in the end, leave us with an old building on our hands.

The conflict between opposing views was escalating bit by bit. I tried to head off what threatened to be the coming storm. I tried to get the "new building" people to see the possibility of fixing the old one. I tried to open the minds of the "old building" people to allow for the idea of replacing it. That way, when the final vote was cast, those on the losing side would be less likely to pick up their marbles and walk. The effort was only mildly successful. JV wouldn't budge.

He gave me an earful. Look at the Europeans! They didn't replace their venerable churches. Some of them were centuries old! There, people had a sense of history. But here in America people had new-edifice complexes. And no roots! Older buildings thoughtlessly bulldozed! Everything had to be shiny and new. And what did the new churches look like? Buildings with abominable functional architecture—and no soul!

I went home. I had a headache. I sat down. Staring out my study window, I rolled back the calendar in my head. I had been through a church building project once before in another city. In reverie I relived the experience. The memories crowded and tumbled through my mind.

My first congregation, comprised of nineteen young families, found itself housed in a store-type building. Its facilities, if not ample, were adequate. But, as people go into buildings, so buildings also go into people, influencing their moods and spirits. So it was that the congregation wanted to move. It is true, of course, that surroundings are not of primary importance in the worship of God. The early Christians worshiped in each other's houses, in the catacombs beneath the city of Rome, and in forest glens. Street-corner meetings are still the Salvation Army's stock-in-trade in many places. People can make too much of the buildings in which they worship. Solomon's temple, whose architect was God himself, was a showplace. We must not, therefore, be critical of the people who labored centuries ago to erect those magnificent cathedrals in Europe that fill us with awe. Still, we must be careful. It is better to have preaching of gold and pulpits of wood rather than the other way around.

Keeping all these thoughts in proper perspective, our small band of nineteen families decided to sell and build. The vote was unanimous. One mother said that her little girl had asked why they didn't go to a church that looked like a church. The chairman of the mission society felt that something with a steeple on it could serve as a better evangelistic tool than a storefront. Another was of the opinion that a new location, where people lived, would insure a future better than the present location on a commercial site and on a busy street. And so the congregation prayed, held its breath, and decided to sell and relocate.

Was it a foolish decision? Too bold? Would it be the death of the church? Where was the money coming from? It was amazing to see all shoulders put to the wheel. Money from the sale of the building was a start. The free use of an area church for worship was a big help, although it forced us to hold worship services at odd hours. A neighborhood was chosen and property purchased. An architect was hired. If all pitched in with painting and more, the cost might be kept down to $75,000. There was much sacrificial giving. There were potlucks and other schemes to make money.

My wife wrote a poem.

Dear Friend,

You must have heard of Dearborn,
that great industrial site.
Within its bounds, there's found my Church,
which spreads the Gospel light.

Our group is small in number,
just nineteen families strong.
The task is great—to preach of Christ
to the surrounding throng.
We seize the opportunity;
to build is now our aim—
a church in this community,
the Gospel to proclaim.
We come in faith and ask your aid.
We know that you will do
all that you can financially,
to make our dream come true.
Just send us dimes or dollars,
whatever you can spare;
and in this worthy cause of faith
you too will have a share.

We mailed the poem everywhere. The response was astonishing—the dimes rolled in through the mail to the tune of slightly over $2,000.

Not all the fundraising projects were equally successful, mine especially. I had heard of a Russian tenor who sang bel canto. He was touring the Midwest. His career had seen better days. Still, putting on a concert to benefit the building fund with him as the star attraction was, I thought, a good idea. I went to work.

He arrived at our doorstep with his wife a whole week early. A scarf tied tightly around his neck protected his precious tonsils. He had just appeared in concert in a church in another city. There had been a freewill offering. He said that he had never seen so many nickels in his life. "Bel Canto" and his wife camped in our spare bedroom and strained our food budget to the breaking point.

Our friend was a late riser—to put it kindly—and was served breakfast in bed by his helpmeet. To soothe his throat he broke his fast each morning with cups of tea mixed with strawberry jam. After he left, we worked hard to get all the spilled sticky strawberry jam out of the carpeting beside the bed. He said that he did not find it necessary to vocalize to keep his voice in shape. Just tea and strawberry jam. That was good, seeing that our newly arrived firstborn needed a lot of sleep. However, our guest did, upon emerging from his room in the morning, sound a high B-flat for ten seconds. It was a sound that unfailingly woke our new son, causing him to vocalize for an hour.

We rented a church with a large sanctuary. We had advertised well, and so the place was filled. Alas, the audience was expecting hymns, not unfamiliar operatic arias. They sat unmoved. After each number I clapped so hard my hands hurt. I wanted a good freewill offering. Not nickels, but dollars. I feared, however, despite Bel Canto's considerable talent, that I had shot myself in the foot.

At one point in the program there was a hitch—an uncoordinated moment between my Bel Canto and the hired pianist. The former corrected the latter with an imperious finger-snap. I could feel the audience's reaction: sympathy for the pianist and disapproval of the hauteur of tenor. The offering followed. I thought sorrowfully, quoting Robert Burns, of how "the best-laid schemes o' mice an' men gang aft a-gley."

At the end of the concert, but too late to influence the collection, my soloist, who had sung in French, Italian, German, Russian, and everything but English, ended with a song the audience recognized and understood—a simple song, ending with the words:

... but come what may,
from day to day,
my heavenly father watches over me.

It was beautiful. It almost rescued the whole evening. But not quite. I led the applause again and wished, but not from the highest motive, that he had sung that hymn before the offering.

That offering, after expenses, netted two hundred dollars for our guest artist and two hundred dollars for the building fund. My wife had made two thousand dollars with a lot less effort! The next morning our guest rose early and disappeared without having had any tea and strawberry jam. He returned mid-morning with a sausage. It became a routine. Every morning he returned with a sausage. At lunch he fed slices of it to our dog, Spotty. Lucky Spotty! I tried to steal a slice from Spotty once. We couldn't afford to go to the butcher.

A week later our guests left. The church made two hundred dollars. "Bel Canto" and wife made two hundred dollars. And, what with food and transportation, my wife and I lost two hundred dollars.

Work continued on our new church building. I helped mornings carrying lumber, mixing concrete, and laying bricks, reserving afternoons and evenings for ministerial labors. Finally the church was completed. We rode in a parade of cars from our temporary worship quarters for a cornerstone-laying ceremony. It contained a document stating, "This church shall stand to serve the coming generations until that day when Christ shall appear upon the day of days. . . ."

Now the little girl could go to a church that looked like a church. Now the chairman of the mission committee could operate from under a steeple, which served as a better missionary tool than a storefront. Now the location was in a residential neighborhood. That was better than being located on a commercial site on a busy street.

The congregation grew. In time it added a Christian school wing. After a while the congregation outgrew the building for which so much had been sacrificed, and they built anew. They sold their church to a Russian Baptist congregation—a building for which, years before, a Russian bel canto tenor had earned $200.

I shook myself out of my reverie. Daydreaming, however pleasant, would not get me anywhere. My thoughts returned to JV. I had met him in college many years before—he was the chairman of the English department. I had enrolled in some of his courses. I still remembered his eloquence when he shared his insights with us on Walt Whitman's *Leaves of Grass*. He was not an ordained minister, but the church had nevertheless given him license to preach because of his ability and fervor. I had served as his driver a number of times when he went preaching here and there. He was as eloquent in the pulpit as he was in the classroom. We became friends. Riding together, conversing together, I discovered what a romanticist he was. He told me one time that if the Christian college where he taught did nothing more than bring two Christian young people together in Christian marriage to establish a Christian home, the whole educational venture was worth it. I could not have imagined in those days that a time would arrive when I would be his preacher.

That day did come. I was not only his preacher, but his pastor. As the latter I was doing all I could to open his mind. If the congregation decided to replace our venerable church building, would he go apoplectic and have a heart attack? His resistance to the idea of a new church was fierce. I sensed that the growing mood of the members for a new sanctuary was becoming an irresistible force. But JV was also an irresistible force—and a very immovable object.

An architect, a friend of the congregation, was engaged to assess the strength of the south wall. He reported that our structure was highly "expendable." Someone thought that meant that the building was worth the "expenditure" of fixing it. The secretary of the church council wrote in the minutes of a meeting that an architect had been hired to "look over the wall." His wording gave me a mental picture of a man standing on a ladder and looking over a wall. I considered suggesting changing the wording to an architect being hired to "inspect" the wall, but I didn't want to be picky.

At a congregational meeting it was decided to ask the architect to render a drawing of what a new church would look like. JV was opposed to such a study. At a well-attended subsequent meeting, a member of the architect's staff showed slides of a pie-shaped structure with a free-standing tower. JV politely referred to it as a monstrosity. The people agreed. Rising to heights of eloquence, JV compared what we had been shown to what we had, and proposed, as before, that we repair what needed repairing and be done with it. Instead, the architect, sensing the mood of the meeting, offered to come with a new rendition. His offer was accepted.

I called on JV the following day. He felt vindicated. The next drawing would probably be even worse. After the next rejection, we would get past this new building fixation and repair our lovely sanctuary. At the next meeting, a new rendering was shown on a slide. After a few stunned seconds, there was loud and sustained applause. There was a feeling that we were all looking at our new church. JV's supporters melted away. He made another speech. He said that the new rendering, albeit attractive, would cost a million dollars of the Lord's money. But the people were no longer with him.

No official decision was made that night. The members were urged to pray and think about it for a month. The final decision would be made at the next congregational meeting. It came. The church council made a recommendation to build the modified Gothic structure, as had been presented at the previous meeting. It was adopted with a strong majority. JV went home. He was crestfallen.

A week before the razing of the old church, the doors were open every day for those who wished to enter, sit, reflect, and meditate. Many of the older people, JV among them, came. When the wrecking ball arrived, there was a large audience gathered across the street. Some wept, JV among them. Services were temporarily held in neighboring churches. The Seventh Day Adventists didn't meet on Sundays. They used their building for society meetings on Sunday evenings. The Presbyterian church down the street did not hold evening services. Both were accommodating.

Meanwhile there was much work to be done. High on the list of priorities was the gathering of gifts and pledges. But who would call on JV? None dared. Some thought it best to omit him from the general canvass. Then two young deacons offered to make the call. They went, some said, where angels feared to tread.

Their report was totally unexpected. JV had invited them into his house. His wife served refreshments. They left with a sizable check and a pledge of much more to come. From JV?

Few really knew that he was a man of some financial substance. "Just a college professor," some said. "Apparently he had made some investments," others said. These conjectures were nothing, however, compared to the wonders expressed at his apparent change of heart. I called on him. I said that I was surprised at his conversion. He replied that he had been opposed to replacing the old structure. But before the final vote earnest prayers had been offered for Divine guidance at meetings, services of worship, and in the homes of the members. God had answered those prayers through the final vote. It was not the answer he had sought. God had led the congregation in another direction. So now it was time for all in the congregation to put their shoulders into it. His devout support was healing and inspiring.

There were a few who left when the vote went against their wishes. There were some who stayed but who refused to give or pledge, but JV was of a different mind. God's will had been sought and God had revealed it. And so, as he said, "Thy will be done." At the cornerstone-laying ceremony, I picked out his beaming face in the crowd. A document was included among other items and placed in the stone, stating, "This church shall stand to serve the coming generations, until that day when Christ shall appear upon the day of days."

JV was pleased with the new sanctuary. He said it was as worshipful as the old. He delighted in showing visitors the new facility. He filled his place in the pew, together with his wife, for many years—until the death of his wife. In failing health, he faced his own end two years later. A saint! I was sure the gates of heaven would be flung wide open to receive him. To my surprise I found him in the last few weeks of his life in a rest home, depressed and despondent. He missed his wife. He missed his church. He missed his study. He missed his books. Worst of all, he had lost the assurance of his salvation. I was mystified. I called on him daily to remind him of God's love for him, but my readings from the Bible and my prayers couldn't reach him.

For many years he had been a leader in the church and in the college. A teacher, a preacher, a man of faith. Why, then, was he so comfortless in the last days of his life? I could only conclude that the devil, who is real, had launched one mighty, last-ditch effort to snatch his soul from the jaws of life. If so, he did not prevail, for in his last few days on earth, JV regained his assurance of faith—and his wonderful smile. I had come for my usual daily visit, wondering what else I could say to revive his spirit. My efforts were not necessary, for as I entered his room, I read the change in his face. He smiled and greeted me with a text on which, a few days later, I based my message at his funeral:

"If we confess our sins, he is faithful and just to forgive our sins, and to cleanse us from all unrighteousness" (1 John 1:9).

17

O Day of Rest and Gladness

Before she met and married C. S. Lewis, Joy Davidman wrote a book on the Ten Commandments. She titled it aptly *Smoke on the Mountain*. Dealing with the fourth commandment (to keep the Sabbath day holy), she wrote imaginatively of a Martian student who had traveled to Earth in a flying saucer to do research for a thesis on comparative anthropology.

As he studied the habits of Earth people, he was particularly struck with their behavior on the first day of the week. He took note of the fact that Earthlings had labeled it "Sun Day"—a twenty-four hour period set aside for the worship of the Sun god. Homage was paid in various ways, such as in sporting events, usually involving a ball of various sizes, all emblematic of the Sun. Others went to beaches where, in brief attire, they exposed themselves to their god, often casting themselves into the waters and afterwards anointing themselves with holy oil. Still others, practicing human sacrifice to the Sun god, enclosed themselves in instruments known as automobiles, in which, aiming at each other at great speeds, they dashed each other to pieces.

Yet among those Earthlings, the Martian student reported, there were heretics. They did not worship the Sun. Instead, they hid themselves from the Sun in steepled buildings with dark windows to keep out the light from the Sun. These steepled buildings, he reported, were generally believed to be places of punishment. The Martian student's thesis on the behavior of Earthlings earned him a Ph.D. in comparative anthropology.

My own praise of the Martian's thesis is measured. He is quite accurate when he emphasizes the great numbers of those who worship the Sun on the day of the Sun. Their number is legion who spend the Sun day on sporting fields, or on beaches, or engaging in highway mayhem. But his understanding of the activities of those who enter steepled buildings on the day of the Sun is sketchy at best, and non-existent at worst. As one who is thoroughly familiar with the activities of those recalcitrants who do not join the frenzy at stadiums or on beaches and expressways, I would like to inform the Martian student that Sunday is, for most of the "heretics," a day of rejoicing. They sing of it:

> Day of all the week the best,
> emblem of eternal rest.

When that Martian student returns to Earth someday, he might find it helpful to read what follows. It is a description, warts and all, of those who enter steepled buildings on Sundays. Come to think of it, it might be helpful not only for the Martian but for churchgoers themselves to read the following portrait.

Sunday morning: Before the service of worship
Some go to church at 11:00 a.m., which Martin Luther King once called "the most segregated hour in the week." Others prefer an earlier time, 9:30 a.m., or even 8:00 a.m. This clears

more of the day for other activities. Indeed, there are some who prefer moving the morning service to the Saturday evening before, thus making room for even more alternatives and possibilities.

Those who prefer the 11:00 a.m. hour like to enjoy an extra snooze in bed. After all, Sunday is supposed to be a day of rest. Then, too, there is time to read the Sunday paper, an institution whose elimination would save great forests of trees throughout the land. There are a few who spend a little time in morning devotions, including prayers for the minister who must shortly lead the churchgoers in worship and in the preaching of the gospel. (Although no polls have been conducted, it seems that these are in the minority.)

Some parents with small children find it a challenge to get all the little ones dressed and ready to pile into the family car to get to the church on time. Speaking of getting dressed, the Martian should know that there are fewer Sunday suits and Sunday dresses than in a former day. The emphasis with some is on more casual attire. Indeed, some who come seem more dressed for beaches than for churches.

As for getting to the church on time, the 11 a.m. service has as many latecomers as does the 8 a.m. service. Many churches appear alarmingly empty five minutes before the scheduled worship hour. Ushers hit their peaks of performance in last minute flurries. Accordingly, the opening hymn, sung by a breathless congregation, hardly rises to the ceiling.

Before Sunday morning services, the clergy are supposedly in their studies, preparing themselves with prayers, devotions, and last minute alterations to their sermons. Those arriving in the pews may be breathless, but those entering pulpits must be composed, poised, and serene. Alas, they are often as harried as the mothers who run from the nursery, where they deposited their darlings, to their sanctuary seats.

Last minute announcements, usually in an illegible scribble, are often thrust into the preacher's hand just before the service. Last-minute emergencies are often the rule rather than the exception. The soloist is late! The organ won't work! The lapel mike battery is dead! In my own case, serving a downtown church, street persons asking to see the minister (but actually looking for a handout) were sometimes brought to me minutes before service time by members eager to do missionary work. Knowing that instant conversions were not likely, I invited them to the service, after which I could speak to them. After church they were usually long gone.

I remember a young couple who were ushered into my study at the last minute. She said she was going to be sick. He was nervous and needed a cigarette. She, thin and pale, fainted and lay at my feet. I dialed 911. I opened the door and called for help. He said he couldn't stand her fainting all the time and that he needed a cigarette. Finally, a deacon came in, having heard my call for help. The man asked him for a cigarette. I handed the deacon the phone and hurried to my post. Could the congregation detect anything as I trotted up the aisle? A minute before I had dealt with a strange woman on my study floor and a man screaming for a cigarette. Now I was moving, ministerially enrobed, to the pulpit—a cleric, presumably prayerfully prepared for his task. Things aren't always what they seem.

Preachers often meet with their elders and deacons for prayer before the service begins. A good custom—though it can get out of hand. There is the temptation sometimes to conduct last minute business. Matters that belong on the agenda of the council meeting are sometimes brought up, briefly discussed, and prematurely decided. Sometimes the prayers offered for a blessing on the service of worship are expanded to include the needs of the whole wide world. This takes time. The minister fidgets, trying to keep his thoughts in line. There was an elder whose prayers before church were interminable. After praying for the preacher, the worship hour, and the worshipers, he would unfailingly branch out to include local needs and the sick, then home missions, then world missions and more. His fellow elders, to say nothing of the preacher, found the length of his prayers burdensome. One morning, as he was about to launch out in his prayer from home missions to world missions, a fellow elder interrupted him and said, "Please, brother, let's stay on this side of the ocean."

When my father was an elder and I was a youngster, I always assumed that the meeting he attended with his fellow elders before church and behind closed doors centered only on the holy and the spiritual. Not so—as I learned when I became a minister. Quite often the talk is about the weather, politics, sporting events, business, and even "the latest" about so-and-so.

In a farming community, so the story goes, the talk in the elders' meeting before church consisted exclusively of complaints about the weather and the anticipated failure of the potato crop. The minister listened to the grumbling for several weeks. Then he decided to teach the elders a lesson. Leading the congregation in intercessory prayer, he did nothing but complain to God about the potato crop. The elders were shocked. How could he? They reprimanded their pastor. It was Thanksgiving Day! Of all days! They stole sheepishly away, however, when the minister said that he had only repeated what he had heard from them.

And so, when God's people heed the call to worship, they come in many moods. They go up to the house of the Lord serene, breathless, tired, prayerful, thoughtless, sleepy, thankful, or preoccupied. Some with hurrying and some with dragging feet. God has a large family. And when his children come to him, the brothers and the sisters are all different. And God loves them all.

Sunday morning: During the service

From earliest years I have always found the traditional beginning of a divine service of worship solemn and impressive. I still do. In the church of my childhood, the first thing that happened was something called the Votum and the Salutation:

> Congregation of the Lord Jesus Christ, Our help is in the name of the Lord who made heaven and earth. Grace be unto you and peace from God the father and the Lord Jesus Christ. Amen.

The people stood to receive this greeting and responded with a psalm of praise. Leading in public worship I have seldom wandered from these opening words, and when I do, it is to say:

> The Lord is in his holy temple.
> Let all the earth keep silence before him.

Opening services of worship with announcements is mood-shattering: "There is a green Buick in the parking lot with the lights on."

This may be considered a necessary piece of information to convey to the assembled faithful, even though it is something less than a Pauline greeting. But other impartations of intelligence, habitually conveyed, are certainly inappropriate for the beginning of the worship hour: "There will be a church picnic in Central Park next Saturday afternoon! Please bring your own silverware."

It has become quite the folksy thing to begin the service with a hearty "Good morning!" greeting to the assembled, complete with a bright and happy smile from the preacher, with a similar response from the gathered. Some like it. I prefer saving such greetings for afterwards when shaking hands at the door. I believe that it is far more fitting to begin with a solemn greeting from the Lord than with a cheery, and sometimes artificial, "Hello" from the preacher. After all, a service of worship is a meeting with God, who greets his people with a blessing.

Ideally, a service of worship consists of acts on the part of God to his people (the votum, the salutation, the reading of the Holy Scriptures, the sermon) and acts on the part of the people to God (the singing of psalms and hymns, the prayers, the offering). Items that do not fit either category should be avoided. The choir, if there is one, fits into the second category, in which trained voices sing to the honor and glory of God on behalf of the congregation. In churches where choirs and soloists are applauded, the people forget that the music was not rendered for their entertainment, but as a praise offering to God. God is the audience, not the people.

Some churches have altered their liturgies with the introduction of praise teams, drums, guitars, and other instruments, or with choruses projected on screens for all to see. Some call these "seeker services." Adaptations are made so that the services are seeker-friendly. Those who are traditionally minded are generally unhappy with such innovations.

I mention all this to inform the student from Mars, should he return, as completely as I can about what goes on in those steepled buildings he knows so little about. They are not places of punishment, as he has been led to believe. He should know that those heretics who refrain from worshiping the Sun on the day of the Sun believe, instead, that it is the day of the Son; the day the Son of God rose from the dead.

> On thee for our salvation,
> Christ rose from depths of Earth.

What happens under those steepled roofs is the worship of God who made all, including Mars, and the preaching of the gospel, which is the good news, and so good it outshines all the bad news of all human history put together! There was a time, when I was small, when I sat in the pew counting organ pipes, or swinging, in imagination, from chandelier to chandelier. I could not assess what tremendous things were taking place around me between God and his people. Today, I am grateful that I was taken, nevertheless, each week, on Sunday, to a steepled building, even though I was not aware that what was going on around me was what I was created for. Today, going to church, I feel sorry for the children playing in the streets, who are not being taken, as I was taken, to weekly services of praise and dedication to the God of the Bible.

Sunday morning: After the service
Living in England for a time, we were often invited after church to someone's house for a glass of sherry. In our churches, Mr. Student from Mars, the beverage is coffee. After the service in the morning, the congregation of believers turns into the Society of the Bean. People stand in small groups sipping their java from little white plastic cups. It is a kind of religious cocktail hour, where the conversation seldom revolves around the sermon just received. It is a time of fellowship, and much admired by those who come from other

traditions where the worshipers go straight home after church.

In the last church I served, the coffee hour came into existence in an unusual manner. There were three members of the congregation whose custom it was to go directly from church to a restaurant a block away for coffee. The elders of the church, plus many in the membership, considered such behavior a breaking of the Sabbath. There were those who had addressed the Three Musketeers, as they were called, with reproving words. To no avail. These—the musketeers—persisted in their evil habit, despite the remonstrations of those who were charged with maintaining the spiritual well-being of all in the congregation.

When I, as the new minister, was apprised of the recalcitrant behavior of the Three Musketeers, and when my ministrations, too, were of no avail, I had what I thought was a brilliant idea. In the spirit of "if you can't lick them, join them," I suggested that we serve coffee in church after the service. Then the Three Musketeers would have no reason to find the brew in a commercial establishment.

The suggestion was debated in the church council. There were those who were unalterably opposed. In the end the suggestion was accepted by a slim margin of votes. The following Sunday, coffee was made available to all after the service. The deacons, concerned with the cost of the new venture, placed collection plates beside the coffee urns. The members of the council who had been unalterably opposed hardened in their opposition when they discovered the collection plates. Had Christ not chased the money changers out of the temple? The following Sunday the collection plates disappeared. But the coffee hour, instituted for the rehabilitation of the Three Musketeers from their errant ways, had no effect. They continued, as their custom was, to go to the restaurant.

The coffee hour became a permanent feature. Not only that, juice and cookies were added. Beside the coffee, there is now also "latté," furnished by the young people for a donation—which really means that the collection plates are back again, albeit in a more palatable form. And so, looking deeply into those plastic coffee cups after church, we see a whole history of "don'ts" (don't sit on Sunday in the coffee shop) turning into "do's" (members now eat out in restaurants at Sunday brunches).

These do's and don'ts are with us late and soon, Mr. Martian. When the bicycle was invented, some pulpits thundered against it as an instrument of Satan wherewith the young people could scamper off to distant places unchaperoned. When the automobile came into vogue, "Sunday joyriding" became a part of the language—a reference to a forbidden exercise. We have already considered the case of the young seminarian who walked more than a Sabbath day's journey rather than sleep another night in a cold room where the bed was too short and the blankets too few.

In my student days, as already observed, I preached every Sunday morning to a small congregation of Presbyterian Calvinists who were death on smoking but went to the movies. I preached on Sunday evenings to a larger congregation of Reformed Calvinists who smoked like chimneys but were death on movies. It would have been disastrous to light a cigarette in the presence of the former or to recommend a good movie to the latter.

I was a product of the Reformed culture in which our fathers placed their cigar butts carefully in their favorite places on the church steps before entering, to be retrieved later (not knowing that we boys had secretly switched them around). But movies were anathema. Years later, the movie ban was removed. Today, when movies are ten times worse, it is permitted to attend. The forbidden movies of the past were silent. Today they are unspeakable. But the banning by the church fathers was wrong—whether movies or coffee in a restaurant. There is such a thing as Christian liberty, a matter Paul addressed in his first letter to the Corinthians.

Sunday afternoon and evening

But how do we spend the parts of our Sunday that fall between services? Surely, if we are to keep the Sabbath holy, there must be some guidelines. There are, and they are simple. We must use the day for worship. We must use the day for rest. And we must not give offense (causing someone to stumble in the Christian walk). The day may certainly be used for the doing of good works.

I received a telephone call one Sunday morning after church. The lady who called and with whom I was not acquainted said that I should know that she had just seen her neighbor, an elder in my church, leaving the house with his wife and a picnic basket. She said that she felt it her duty to inform me that they were obviously breaking the Sabbath. The elder in question was a very godly man. I managed to remain cordial in my phone conversation with a woman I considered a snoop. It was hard not to tell her to mind her own business. I found out later that the elder in question, together with his wife, had been in the process of bringing a hot Sunday dinner to a shut-in. My informant was of the same stripe as the Pharisees in the New Testament. Jesus reprimanded those unholy spies. He didn't like their hypocritical shock when a man pulled his donkey out of a ditch on the Sabbath.

Having observed all of this, I regret that I must nevertheless confess to the student from Mars that numbers of those who visit steepled buildings on Sundays join those other worshipers on beaches, in sports stadiums, and on break-neck highways after the service. The increasing victory of "Sunday" over "Sonday" is regrettable. I am reminded of a sermon I heard many years ago on the fourth commandment.

It was delivered by a Presbyterian minister from Scotland. He told us about his boyhood— how, on the first day of the week, dressed in Sunday best, he walked behind his parents, silently and solemnly, to the "kirk." Three times a day! Between services his activities were restricted. His in-depth description had everyone in the congregation feeling sorry for him. He went on, however, to contrast his Sundays of old with the Sundays of his listeners. He said some of them had their golf clubs in the trunks of their cars, ready to head for the golf links after church. He said some of them had their beachwear with them ready to head for the ocean shore after church. He said some of them had dates to meet friends after church in restaurants here and there. He added that few of them would be back for evening vespers.

He paused. Then he said, "I think we were all better off when we had those Sundays of my boyhood times." End of sermon! After which some of his hearers headed for the links, the beaches, the restaurants, and the highways.

But some came back for evening vespers.

Was the Scot too dour? Perhaps. The faithful are numberless. Still, since we are furnishing the Martian with information regarding those who sit in steepled buildings, we must be honest and objective.

There is a beautiful picture somewhere of a congregation at Sunday worship. The preacher looks like an Old Testament prophet. The choir members appear like other-worldly creatures—angels above Bethlehem skies. In the pews, the mothers all beam like it is Mothers' Day, and their daughters look pure and virginal. The fathers, pillars all, seem destined for sainthood and their sons for seminary, while all the huggable little ones are cherubs straight out of medieval paintings.

The face of any parish is far less beautiful, a fact that makes God's love for his children appear all the greater. God's family is a grand mix of strong and weak, of fervent and lukewarm. Open the doors and see all the people, and note that even the best of them have warts. I have tried to show you some of them, Mr. Martian, in order to give you an untouched portrait. You may wonder, therefore, how those steepled houses stay in business. The truth is that the church persists, not *because* of its people, but *in spite* of them.

This is a mystery indeed. If you would know the answer—in order to make your thesis complete—I invite you to read on.

I Love Thy Church, O Lord

I was ordained into the ministry of the gospel more than fifty years ago. For more than half a century I have preached and pastored in a fast-moving and fast-changing age. Sometimes I am asked whether I would do it all over again, if given the chance to relive my life. I can say, truthfully, that given the chance I would gladly do it all over again.

I had a friend, a contemporary, who went into the ministry. After three years he left the rolls of the clergy to go on to other things. Whenever the calling of the ministry surfaced in conversation he would say, "Been there, done that," or words to that effect. But just as travelers can't see England in three days, no matter how many miles they ride in chartered buses, so no one can do ministry in three years. It takes a lifetime. As a matter of fact, just as one begins to catch on a bit as to how it is done, it is time to retire.

Even so, having taken more than fifty years to go from ordination to emeritation—which my dictionary tells me is not a word—there is a sense in which I can legitimately say that I've "been there and done that." Indeed, though in lesser measure, I am still doing it.

However, the ministry, like life itself, is not always a bowl of cherries. It requires more than just one hour on Sunday mornings and another on Sunday evenings. Nor is it the sheltered life some say it is. To do it justice requires long hours, patience, and a strong hide.

There are rewards, but there are also trials and anxious hours and days. Less than a year after I was launched into the ministry, the membership of my small congregation plummeted before it built up again. I worried sleeplessly about whether I had chosen the right occupation. And when television was in its infancy, the members of my flock, good people all, debated whether or not to approve of the set I owned and the antennae which stood boldly on the roof of the parsonage for all the world to see. I wondered at the chances of my survival in the ministry. Congregations can be cruel—sometimes consciously, but more often unknowingly. An ex-clergyman, who went from preaching to painting houses, said to me, "The first five years I could do nothing wrong in their eyes; the next five years I could do nothing right."

I remember an older woman, a member of my flock, who was distant at best and hostile at worst. I had heard that she had little use for me because, in her view, I was a liberal. We did shake hands at the door after services, but her hand always felt like a cold dead fish. She never looked at me as she gave me her gift from the sea. She never saw the smile with which I was trying to win her heart. I half succeeded, because one Sunday morning, with a dead fish in my hand, I saw her pause, look at me, and say, "Well, I think you're getting a little better." That was as far as she could bend. Her principles prevented any further pliancy toward me. I was told by others, a few years later, that she no longer disliked me, although to say that she approved of me would be going too far. And so the dead fish in my hand never came to life.

Having initially expressed her disapproval of me, she had painted herself into a corner and wouldn't even try to get out. Her pride prevented her.

I wish I knew how many hours I have spent making sermons. But did preaching them do any good? How many people listen or remember? The Old Testament prophet Jeremiah, whose lips were touched by God, preached for more than forty-two years without a single convert. Only a preacher can guess how many demons must have sat on Jeremiah's shoulder telling him that he was wasting his breath. Those demons have sat on my shoulders too. When they did, an old story buoyed me up. A man complained about his wife's cooking. He said that he had eaten her meals for fifty years and couldn't remember a single one of them. "Perhaps not," was the reply, "but for fifty years they have sustained and nourished you."

When, years ago, good people were debating the removal of my television set, I thought of the history of controversy in the church—some of it necessary, but a lot of it ridiculous. I prize the memory of the church of my childhood. Next to my Christian home, it was the most important thing in my life. But the minor controversies that were always boiling and sometimes polarizing the members were often the little foxes that were spoiling the vines. Bobbed hair. Playing cards. Movies. Dancing. The common cup versus the individual cup. Sabbath observance. The permissibility of choirs in a service. Christian or public schools. These and other deadly serious issues often tested the ties that bound. Sometimes those ties broke.

By the time I became an ordained clergymen, the issues, although altered by the times, still persisted. Should the Deity be addressed as "thou" or "you"? Could women wear pantsuits to church? What about long hair on men? When I introduced responsive readings into our church services, some turned the innovation into an issue. More recently, alterations in liturgy have disturbed the peace of the church. Musical offerings please some and offend others. The pot is always boiling.

Nor are annoyances limited to congregational life. What goes on at the denominational level can be equally disillusioning. Committees, boards, synods, and general assemblies are all necessary for denominations to function. Yet they are not without their intrasquabbles, tensions, alignments, and power plays. Do you suppose that Pastor A who is among the "outs" will ever be asked to serve with the "ins" on Committee B? Not on your tintype! It is good that the majority of the membership is unaware of the politics, in the bad sense, that can exist in the ecclesiastical world. I have been behind the scenes. Or spell it "behind the seens." The church is not always what it seems.

If any of this makes anyone wonder why I would do it all over again, then it is good to remember that candor and love are not mutually exclusive. I do love the church despite its warts and failures. It is made up of people, all of whom have their foibles and weaknesses. Few escape at least a dab from the brush of hypocrisy. All are human. It is good for the idealists among us to remember that even the most sainted, in pew or pulpit, put their pants on one leg at a time. All are sinners.

Like me.

True, it is better to hear the harsh truth from an enemy than to hear it sugar-coated from a friend. But better than both is truth spoken in love.

In all of these disillusioning aspects of the church I have found a sense of humor to be indispensable. Somewhere I have a cartoon of a preacher in a pulpit. It is a rear view, a choir member's view. From the front the preacher looks very proper. Impressive. Ministerial. You can tell. But from the back you get a different picture. His robe is open, exposing his street clothes. His pipe is partially in view in his rear pocket. One shirttail is half out of his trousers, and one end of his suspenders is loose for lack of a button. From the front he cuts quite a figure. But from the back he looks like a vulnerable mortal. I laugh when I look at that picture because that rear view, so much more than the front view, is a picture of us all.

"O wad some Pow'r the giftie gie us," wrote the Scottish bard Robert Burns, "to see oursels as others see us!" With Bible in hand, we get a peek at how God sees us. There is none righteous! But since our foibles and weaknesses are placed in focus by a loving heavenly Father, we should consider one another's shortcomings in that same spirit.

The saints have their idiosyncrasies. Some are hard to live with. Pettiness is no stranger among them. Often, with planks in their eyes, they concentrate on the slivers in others eyes. Nor are preachers exempt. Some seek to build kingdoms around themselves. Some preen in pulpits. Some stand on tiptoes, impressively proclaiming their vast knowledge of the trigonometry of life when what their people need to hear is that two plus two equal four.

God's people, though they have their weaknesses, also have their strengths. Those who wonder at the survival of the church through the centuries should consider the positives. When calling on the sick with a word of comfort, I cannot count the times that I received more than I brought. I marvel at those who live lives of quiet devotion: an aged woman, devoting the entire morning of every day to praying for the forty people on her prayer list; a widow, whose hobby was growing flowers, making anonymous gifts of lovely bouquets every week to the lonely in local hospitals and rest homes; a man who lived modestly so that he could give his monthly pension money for the support of orphans in third world countries.

A preacher friend of mine survived the German occupation of his country. Afterwards, he shared some of his experiences with me. A few of the members of his church showed a lack of perseverance in the faith when the going got tough. What amazed and blessed my friend were those, some of whom he had considered to be living on the periphery of the church, who surprised him with the courage of their convictions, and with the steel in their Christian commitment. Their loyalty was an inspiration to him, and, as he told me the story, to me.

The numbers of the truly godly multiplied in my mind as my own pastoral experiences and insights increased. For starters, there was Mr. A.

Mr. A. never missed a church service, and the offering plate never passed him in vain. Diligent in worship, he was also diligent in his work as a store clerk. His employer once told me that he would trust Mr. A. with his life. Yet, although he was a trusted employee and a faithful Christian, his rewards were few. There were no opportunities for promotion where he labored. He lived unheralded and unnoticed by all, except for his family and friends. Others around him climbed the ladder of success while he remained on a lower rung. He was, nevertheless, contented with his lot. More than that. He was an uncomplaining and grateful Christian.

The mission committee of the church, of which Mr. A. was a member, proposed a series of evangelistic meetings with speakers from various walks of life. A successful businessman, who had made it big in banking, was proposed as one of the speakers. He accepted, and on the appointed evening gave his testimony by way of telling his story. The secret of his success, we were informed, lay in a biblical formula he had put together for himself, part of which was found in Proverbs 22:29: "Seest thou a man diligent in his business? He shall stand before kings . . . " Our speaker informed us that he was an example of the literal truth of that text, for he had been diligent in his business—as a result of which he had had an audience with the king of Denmark. Or was it Sweden? I forget.

I was standing in the back of the sanctuary as we all viewed this living, shining example of Proverbs 22:29. Directly in front of me sat Mr. A. I watched him and wondered what he was thinking. He was, to me, the personification of Christian diligence in home, at church, and at work. But I doubted whether he would ever appear before the king of Denmark. Or was it Sweden? I forget. I began to feel some resentment toward the speaker for his insensitive and arrogant self-praise. I began to take issue in my mind with his interpretation of Proverbs 22:29. Perhaps the speaker was, indeed, diligent in his work. But nobody on earth could have been as unflaggingly diligent as Mr. A.

At the end of Mr. A's earthly span, I buried him. The king of Denmark (or was it Sweden?) did not attend his funeral. But God was there. I could almost hear him saying, "Well done, good and faithful servant." There was no article in the paper marking his passing, except in the heavenly press. To this day I can see him listening to the banker with joy in his heart because the banker had received his reward and had stood before a king. His was a better reaction than mine. I'm sure Mr. A. never wondered why he had not stood before the king of Denmark. Or was it . . . never mind.

To this day Mr. A. is one of my heroes of the faith. And one of my examples.

Or take Mr. B. He was erudite. The reputation of his learning had spread to many college campuses and universities in the land. I stood in awe of him. Often when preaching I would see him in his accustomed place and think that he should be in the pulpit and that I should occupy his pew. On Sundays he sat at my feet, when I should have been sitting at his.

When I shared this thought with him one day, he put me at ease at once. I should have known that this would be his reaction, for he was ever a man of kindness and humility. But if he sat at my feet on Sundays, I sat at his on as many Thursday evenings as I could spare, for I had a standing invitation to his house. I can still see him sitting in his chair, forever lighting his pipe, a dozen open books (in as many languages) spread on the floor around him. If I volunteered a thought that was far from bright, he would never put me down. Instead, he would observe, "There is something to what you say," and then proceed to redirect my thoughts.

I was with him in the hospital the night his wife died. He was deeply saddened as I led him, at two o'clock in the morning, to his car in the parking lot. I offered to drive him home. He didn't hear what I had said. At two o'clock in the morning the city is at its quietest. I wanted to put my arm around him, but it didn't seem the right thing to do at that moment, for he was lost in reverie. Indeed, I thought he had forgotten me. It was a beautiful night. The heavens were alive with stars. He seemed to be studying them. At last, he stirred. He looked at me, then up again into space, and said, "Pastor, she's up there now." I agreed.

He drove himself home.

I have never forgotten that moment. He was too well-educated, too well-informed, to believe in a three-story universe. The world is round and revolves. When we point up, then do so again twelve hours later, we end up pointing in opposite directions. Even so, Mr. B., whose knowledge far surpassed my own, said, "She's up there now." It was an expression of childlike faith on the part of the most informed and intelligent mind I had ever met.

Mr. B. is one of my heroes of the faith. And one of my examples.

So is Mr. C. He was a character. He had been a theological professor, but he had lost his position for, allegedly, going to a movie—a thing *verboten* in his day. Unemployed, he was hard put to furnish bread for the table. He worked for a time as an elevator operator in a downtown store. His head was as bald as the proverbial billiard ball. Driving home from church very late on a bitterly cold January night, I passed him as he was walking, hatless, on the sidewalk. I stopped, invited him into my car, and brought him home. I said that if he stayed out like that very long his brains would freeze. He said he was hatless because his brains needed cooling off. I asked whether they had sufficiently cooled. He said, "Not yet," and explained that on a cold night most of your body heat passes out of the body through the top of the head if you are hatless. With his body heat escaping through the top of his head his brains were still hot from the passing escaping heat.

He was stone deaf and his eyesight was poor. He said that if he had his choice he would rather be blind than deaf. (This was a time before we used such words as *sightless* and *hearing impaired.*) When I disagreed, he said that I should change places with him for a week, and then I could speak more intelligently.

He wanted the tapes of my sermons. He said he had a machine that could amplify my voice. When I called at his home I saw the tape strung out all over the living room from light fixture to curtain rods to picture hooks and crisscrossing back to the light fixture. It looked like the room had been decorated for a birthday party. He said he had dropped my sermon by accident into his coffee and that he was hanging it out to dry. Knowing that he would never be able to put it together again, I gave him another copy of the tape. "How was it?" I asked him the following Sunday. He said it was pretty dry and that he should have dropped it into the coffee. Hilarious!

He complained that when he sat up too late in his study, well past midnight, his wife would force him to go to bed by pulling on his hair. When I pointed out to him that he had no hair, he showed me some at the base of his neck. He said pulling on them was painful. I said he could shave them off and then he could stay in his study all night. He replied that, in view of the fact that he had no hair on his head, he prized those few he had at the base of his neck.

I was fascinated. He was one of a kind. Hidden behind his idiosyncrasies there was a brilliant scholar. He was a historian. Church history was his specialty. He could dwell on any part of it as if giving an eyewitness account. Seeing his financial need, a fellow member of the church, a publisher, himself quite a character, gave Mr. C. an advance in royalty to produce a textbook on the church in history. When his writings were not forthcoming with sufficient speed, an incentive was given, small advances for twenty pages a week. Thereafter the twenty pages a week materialized, albeit in very large handwriting. Eventually the book was completed, a very rewarding volume mined from a lifetime of study and research, yet written in such a way as to keep in mind the needs and the capacities of the boys and girls for whom it was written. A textbook! It became a source of knowledge for generations of students, and is, even today, a most rewarding read.

What I found most fascinating about Mr. C. was his quizzical nature and his teasing eyes. His manner suggested that amusing secrets were attached to the deepest theological questions as well as the simplest things in life. Nothing was dull. Everything was interesting. Even the most obvious truths were filled with alluring mysteries. I learned from him to see all aspects of life in deeper dimensions.

Mr. C., too, became one of my heroes of the faith. And I learned from him.

I remember a conversation with Mr. C. that well serves the purpose of this book. He said that when we think of church history, we think in terms of the St. Augustines, the Luthers, the Calvins, the Zwinglis. We think in terms of Origen, Justin, Polycarp, and more. And well we should. We think of popes and movements and church councils—again, well we should. But, he added, we must also think of the people "as the sands of the sea" and "as the stars of the heavens"—the seed of Abraham. The numberless anonymous. For church history is much more than the stories of St. Augustine, Luther, and Calvin.

Abraham Kuyper (noted Dutch theologian, author, editor, politician, and prime minister) spoke of the "little people" and their importance. Only the Lord knows the stories they wrote with their lives in Christian service. The names of those who died in the Roman coliseum are unknown to us, but they were all people like us. Political climates were often unfriendly for Christians, yet they multiplied, as in China today. Unlike horticulture, which teaches that plants do not thrive or even survive in unfriendly conditions, church history shows that Christians do, and have. But the names on their gravestones, if indeed they had gravestones, have been erased by the wind and weather of time.

And what about the millions who lived uneventfully, and who are now lost and forgotten in the mists of history, yet who, in their day, carried the church forward to the next generation—people with weaknesses but also strengths. It took the Toms,

Dicks, and Harrys, Annes and Esthers, through all the generations (plus their nickels and, more importantly, their faith, hope, and love) to build the church.

Our forefathers came to a strange land in a new world. They lived in sod huts. They froze to death in the wintertime. They were eaten by mosquitoes in the summertime. The infant mortality rate was high among them. Illnesses often decimated their ranks. Yet with their pennies they built the churches and the schools we have inherited from them and which we enjoy in relative affluence. What an inspiration they are! What heroes they were!

The apostle Paul wrote to the Christians in Corinth (1 Cor. 1:26f.) that "not many wise men after the flesh, not many mighty, not many noble are called; But God hath chosen the foolish things of the world to confound the wise; and God hath chosen the weak things of the world to confound the things which are mighty; and base things of the world and things which are despised, hath God chosen, yea, and things which are not, to bring to nought things that are; That no flesh should glory in his presence."

God could have chosen his angels to spread the gospel and do the work of the church. Presumably they would have done, and would still be doing, a much better job. But instead, God chose the little people, the weak, the nonentities, in vast numbers. A grand mix. The Mr. As, Bs, Cs, and Mrs. or Ms. Ds, Es, Fs, and so on through the alphabet endlessly.

However! When we examine the church, the oldest institution in history, against which the gates of hell shall not prevail, and when we consider the mystery of its longevity, the answer is not that it lives because of the strengths of the faithful. The answer to the endurance of the church is found in the answer to another question, namely—whose is it?

The church belongs to Jesus Christ. It is, indeed, his body on earth. He is its head. The church is the bride of Christ, and no groom is more protective. Although he tries, Satan cannot wrest it away. Jesus Christ promised his bride the gift of the Holy Spirit to her through the ages. That Holy Spirit did come upon the church on a day we call Pentecost, and he has remained with it to the present. And so the church is neither destroyed by our weakness nor maintained by our strength. The church perseveres in spite of us and because of him. The perseverance of the saints should rather be labeled the perseverance of the Holy Spirit.

It is said that Karl Barth, the famous Swiss theologian, was once asked for a proof of the truth of the Bible and of the Christian religion. A simple answer was requested. It is said that, after reflection, he answered with two words: "The Jews." It was a thought-provoking reply. The mystery of the existence of the Jews today is a mystery indeed. No people have been more hounded through the centuries, more maligned, more exterminated. Humanly speaking, they should be an extinct species, forever gone like the dodo bird. Yet here they are. Still a presence to be reckoned with. No secular historian can present an acceptable answer to this riddle. The solution can only be found with the Bible in hand. The Jews are God's indestructible chosen race.

Karl Barth might well have answered another way. Instead of saying "the Jews" he could just as well have said "the church." It, too, has been persecuted through the centuries, perhaps never more than today in certain parts of the world. But, like the farmer said when his crops were overrun with a wave of locusts, "Where you stamp one out, two more appear." So it is with the church. The illustration is not the best, for locusts are a plague and the church is not. Its members are the light of the world and the salt of the earth. Let those who deny the truths of Christianity wrestle with the arresting fact of the perseverance of the church. Some of the "wise" of the eighteenth and nineteenth centuries predicted the total disappearance of the church from the face of the earth by the end of the twentieth century. The truth is that it will still be here in the twenty-first, and it will remain for as long as it takes Jesus Christ to come again.

It was Jesus who said that those who comprise the church are the light of the world and the salt of the earth. The late Dr. Clarence McCartney enlarged on these words memorably. He said, "The poorest church building, a mere wooden shack, with broken windows, a whining organ, and bare benches, and scattered worshipers, and a dull preacher, is yet a far more significant fact in my community or city than a library with its thousands of volumes, or a bank with its Grecian columns and its vaults bursting with gold and silver."

Thomas Chalmers once said, "The world is bad enough with the church—what would it be without it?"

A secular sociologist, earlier in our history, observed that where there were the most problems there were the fewest churches.

So—

Open the doors and see all the people under the steeple! A grand mix. Hezekiah. Two sisters who didn't get along together but who loved each other nevertheless. A catechism class. A gas station operator. Building committees. A preacher with old sermons. A lady with a preference for green blankets. Old cronies—one liberal, one conservative. A husband locked out. Another—a wife, calling the preacher for help. Children. A lady who wore cucumbers. A penny-pinching groom. A police lieutenant. A man and a quiz contest. A man of royal descent. A man and his daughter. A seminary student who could have used some snow shoes. A man who fought for an expendable building. Three coffee drinkers. Someone who did not stand before a king. A brain who looked beyond the stars. A man who hung a sermon out to dry. When these and more gather under the steeple, they sing, "Like a mighty army moves the church of God." But they don't exactly give the appearance of a mighty army. And yet, they are an indestructible lot. And when they gather for worship—how good and pleasant is the sight of families walking down the aisles to their pews. Single folk sliding into their seats. A newborn child, fearfully and wonderfully made, known to God already in the womb, presented for the sacrament of baptism. A bride and groom uniting their lives, speaking their vows. Choirs and congregations lifting voices in psalms, hymns, and spiritual songs. The sense of the Holy Spirit moving within and among God's people. The greetings at the door. The meetings through the week. Young people making professions of faith while parents and grandparents watch with tear-brimmed eyes. The comfort from the Scriptures at a funeral. The benediction. The fellowship. The convert with a shining smile. The table of the Lord. The surpassing beauty of it all!

This is a church.
This is a steeple.
Open the doors.
See all the people!